- Go to **awmi.net/sg441** to download PDFs of the following resources for each lesson in this study guide:
    - Outlines
    - Discipleship Questions
    - Scriptures
- Share as many copies as you'd like.
- These documents are not for resale.

How to Become a

Water Walker

Lessons in Faith

Study Guide

Andrew Wommack

Unless otherwise indicated, all Scripture quotations are taken from the *King James Version* of the Bible.

How to Become a Water Walker Study Guide
ISBN: 978-1-59548-285-3

Copyright © 2015 by Andrew Wommack Ministries Inc.
PO Box 3333
Colorado Springs CO 80934-3333

Published by Andrew Wommack Ministries Inc.

awmi.net

TABLE OF CONTENTS

How to Use Your Study Guide

Whether you are teaching a class, leading a small group, discipling an individual, or studying on your own, this study guide is designed for you! Here's how it works:

Each lesson consists of the **Lesson** text, **Outline, Teacher's Guide, Discipleship Questions, Answer Key,** and **Scriptures**. Some studies also have additional information.

Outline for Group Study:

I.   If possible, briefly review the previous lesson by going over the **Answer Key/ Teacher's Guide** answers for the **Discipleship Questions/Teacher's Guide** questions.

II. Read the current **Lesson** text or **Teacher's Guide** aloud.
A.   Be sure that each student has a copy of the **Outline**.
B.   While the **Lesson** text or **Teacher's Guide** is being read, students should use their **Outlines** to follow along.

III. Once the **Lesson** text or **Teacher's Guide** is read, facilitate discussion and study using the **Discipleship Questions/Teacher's Guide** questions (all questions are the same).
A.   Read one question at a time.
B.   The group should use their **Outlines** to assist them answering the questions.
C.   Have them read aloud each specifically mentioned scripture before answering the question.
D.   Discuss the answer/point from the **Lesson** text as desired.
E.   As much as possible, keep the discussion centered on the scriptures and the **Lesson** text or **Teacher's Guide** points at hand.
F.   Remember, the goal is understanding (Matt. 13:19).
G.   One individual should not dominate the discussion; instead, try to draw out the quieter ones for the group conversation.
H.   Repeat the process until all of the questions are discussed/answered.

Materials Needed:
Study guide, Bible, and enough copies of the **Outline, Discipleship Questions,** and **Scriptures** for each student. (PDFs of the **Outlines, Discipleship Questions,** and **Scriptures** can be downloaded via the URL located on the first page of this study guide.)

Outline for Personal Study:

    I.   Read the current **Lesson** text or **Teacher's Guide**.
    A.   Read additional information, if provided.
    B.   Meditate on the given scriptures, as desired.

    II.   Answer the corresponding **Discipleship Questions/Teacher's Guide** questions.

    III.   Check your work with the **Answer Key/Teacher's Guide** answers.

Materials Needed:

    Study guide, Bible, and a writing utensil.

THE LORD SPOKE

LESSON 1

In Matthew 14, Jesus fed five thousand men with five loaves and two fish. Taking into account the women and children present, there could have been upward of ten, fifteen, or even twenty thousand people! Then, immediately after this miracle...

> Jesus constrained his disciples to get into a ship, and to go before him unto the other side, *while he sent the multitudes away. [23] And when he had sent the multitudes away, he went up into a mountain apart to pray: and when the evening was come, he was there alone. [24] But the ship was now in the midst of the sea, tossed with waves: for the wind was contrary.*
>
> Matthew 14:22-24, emphasis mine

Notice how the Word says that Jesus constrained His disciples to get into the ship and go to the other side. He didn't tell them to go only halfway and then drown. This is important!

GOD'S WORD

These words about going to the other side were spoken by the Creator (Col. 1:16). Jesus is the one who spoke that very lake into existence. All of His words carry that same creative power. When the Lord says something, there's a purpose for it. He never wastes His breath. He never speaks an idle word. If the Lord has ever told you something, He meant every single bit of it. Everything God says is significant!

The disciples didn't think about who had told them to do this.

> *In the beginning was the Word, and the Word was with God, and the Word was God.... [3] All things were made by him; and without him was not any thing made that was made.*
>
> John 1:1 and 3

This passage goes on to say that Jesus is that Word.

God spoke everything into existence, and He did it through Jesus. The Lord upholds *"all things by the word of his power"* (Heb. 1:3).

The entire world is held together by the integrity of His Word:

> *And by him all things consist.*
>
> Colossians 1:17

The God who created everything physical—including the wind, waves, and the water they were about to encounter—was Jesus. Jesus was the parent force, and He said to get in and go to the other side! Apparently, the disciples didn't understand whom they were dealing with.

OVERWHELMED BY CIRCUMSTANCES

The disciples had glimpsed who Jesus was, but they weren't keeping it foremost in their thoughts. Although Peter had confessed a couple of chapters earlier, *"Thou art the Christ, the Son of the living God"* (Matt. 16:16), he wasn't thinking like that now. As a matter of fact, the Bible says the disciples were shocked to see Jesus walk on the water because their hearts were hardened. They hadn't considered—meditated, pondered, thought on—the miracle they had just seen.

> *They were sore amazed in themselves beyond measure, and wondered. [52] For they considered not the miracle of the loaves: for their heart was hardened.*
>
> Mark 6:51-52

If they had really thought about who had told them to do this and what He had just done, they wouldn't have been so overwhelmed. This Man had just taken five loaves and two fish and fed almost twenty thousand people. Not only that, there was more left over when everyone was finished than what He began with! If the disciples had been focused on that miracle, they wouldn't have been shocked to see Jesus perform another one. They would have been expecting it. Or they could have taken Jesus' words, believed them, and then stilled the storm or walked on the water to the other side. That's what the Lord wanted them to do.

In the midst of the storm, the disciples could have stood on the Lord's word to them and said, "He didn't tell us to go to the middle of the lake and run the risk of drowning!" The disciples had already seen Jesus command the wind and waves to cease (Mark 4:39). They could have drawn on that same example and used their faith to calm the present storm, as they had seen Jesus do before.

You might say, "But Andrew, this was a severe storm!" Most people would give the disciples a total pass on this and sympathize with them completely. But they weren't the disciples of a mere man, and the instructions they had received to go to the other side weren't just powerless words. They had what they needed to accomplish Jesus' instructions; they just reverted to being carnal and forgot all the supernatural lessons taught that day.

The Sea of Galilee is only 7.5 miles wide and 12.75 miles long. I've been there before. We went out on the water in a tourist vessel called "The Jesus Boat," and I taught about the things recorded in the Gospels that happened there. It was a fun experience! However, the Sea of Galilee isn't a big sea, and the disciples' destination was only about 4 miles away.

"WHY ARE YOU FEARFUL?"

The disciples boarded the boat and set out from shore sometime around sunset, which could have been anytime from 6 to 8 o'clock in the evening (Mark 6:47). Yet here it was in the fourth watch—sometime between 3 and 6 in the morning—when Jesus came to them (Mark 6:48). So, in seven to twelve hours, they had covered only two miles, or what normally would have been an hour's trip. Most people would say, "You can't fault them. Look, the winds were really bad!" But again, that's because they magnify physical, natural things instead of God.

When the Lord spoke to the disciples, He didn't compliment them or say, "Guys, I'm sorry. It's My fault. I shouldn't have left you out on the sea by yourself. I'm responsible. I should have been there and done something." No, that wasn't the Lord's response. He expected them to do better than they did. He expected them to make it to the other side, just as He had instructed them. Likewise, I believe the Lord expects us to do better than most of us are doing. We have His promises but just aren't believing them.

Many people identify with the disciples and say, "I understand exactly how they felt. It's hard to maintain your faith when you're in the midst of a storm!" Although the Lord understands and has compassion on us, that isn't normal. It may be normal according to those who don't believe God, but it isn't the normal Christian life.

We need to recognize and focus on whom we serve, the command He's given us, and what He's already done. God didn't call us to lose the battle and be a failure. He didn't call us to die of sickness or to live in such poverty that we can't fulfill His will. God made us world overcomers (1 John 5:4)! We need to meditate on the promises and words that God has spoken to us. Instead of being overcome by our problems, we can overcome our problems by His promises.

When Jesus spoke to the disciples, He didn't tell them, "Go part of the way. Then, if there's absolute calm, you might make it. But if a storm comes up, you guys have had it!" No, He told them to go to the other side. They had a word from Creator God, and if they had put absolute faith in that, they could have stood in the face of that storm and defied it. They could have walked on the water like Jesus and Peter did!

IN OVER YOUR HEAD, OR PLAYING IT TOO SAFE?

This instance of Jesus walking on the water to His disciples is recorded in three of the Gospels (Matt. 14:22-33, Mark 6:45-52, and John 6:15-21). John's account shows us another important detail:

> *Then they willingly received him* [Jesus] *into the ship: and immediately the ship was at the land whither they went.*
>
> John 6:21, brackets mine

The disciples and Jesus were translated two miles to the other side. What a miracle! The boat and all its inhabitants were instantly transported to the other side, where Jesus originally told them to go. It's very possible that if they had stood and believed, this would have happened for them even before Jesus showed up on the scene.

When God commands something, everything in creation has to bow its knee to what He says. The only reason this doesn't happen for us is because few people really believe. We get swamped by the storms of life. If we would get this attitude of faith, it would change our experience. If the disciples would've had this attitude, they would have had a totally different experience.

> *But the ship was now in the midst of the sea, tossed with waves: for the wind was contrary.*
>
> Matthew 14:24

At times, God will tell us to do things that go against the normal flow of nature. God lives in the supernatural realm, and if we are truly following Him, we will too. If we aren't supernatural, we're just superficial. The Lord wants us to move into the unlimited, supernatural realm with Him.

The Lord may have laid things on your heart that just seem absolutely impossible. The wind, waves, and storms of life may be coming against you and it may look like you could drown. Instead of accomplishing God's will, it may appear as if you're going to die in the attempt. If you haven't ever been in a situation like that where you've gotten in over your head, it's probably because you're playing it too safe. Get out on the limb. That's where all the fruit grows. Step out of the boat and start walking on the water!

Outline

I.   After Jesus fed five thousand men with five loaves and two fish, look what happened:

> *Jesus constrained his disciples to get into a ship, and to go before him unto the other side, while he sent the multitudes away. [23] And when he had sent the multitudes away, he went up into a mountain apart to pray: and when the evening was come, he was there alone. [24] But the ship was now in the midst of the sea, tossed with waves: for the wind was contrary.*
>
> Matthew 14:22-24, emphasis mine

   A. Jesus' words about going to the other side were spoken by the Creator (Col. 1:16).

   B. He is the one who spoke that very lake into existence—all of His words carried that same creative power.

   C. If the Lord has ever told you something, He meant every single bit of it.

   D. The disciples didn't think about who had told them to do this.

   E. Jesus was the parent force, and He said, "Get in and go to the other side!"—the disciples didn't understand whom they were dealing with.

II. The disciples had glimpsed who Jesus was, but they weren't keeping it foremost in their thoughts.

   A. If they had really thought about who had told them to do this, they wouldn't have been so overwhelmed.

   B. In the midst of the storm, the disciples could have stood on the Lord's word to them and said, "He didn't tell us to go to the middle of the lake and run the risk of drowning!"

   C. They had what they needed to accomplish Jesus' instructions; they just reverted to being carnal and forgot all the supernatural lessons taught that day.

III. Most people would say, "You can't fault the disciples. Look, the winds were really bad!" but again, that's because they magnify physical, natural things instead of God.

A. When the Lord spoke to the disciples, He didn't say, "Guys, I'm sorry; I shouldn't have left you out on the sea by yourself."

B. I believe the Lord expects us to do better than most of us are doing; we have His promises but just aren't believing them.

C. Many people identify with the disciples and say, "I understand exactly how they felt; it's hard to maintain your faith when you're in the midst of a storm!"

D. Although the Lord understands and has compassion on us, that isn't normal; it may be normal according to those who don't believe God, but it isn't the normal Christian life.

E. We need to recognize and focus on whom we serve, the command He's given us, and what He's already done.

F. Instead of being overcome by our problems, we can overcome our problems by His promises.

G. If the disciples had put absolute faith in what Jesus said, they could have walked on the water.

IV. John's account of Jesus walking on the water shows us another important detail:

Then they willingly received him [Jesus] into the ship: and immediately the ship was at the land whither they went.

John 6:21, brackets mine

A. The boat and all its inhabitants were instantly transported to the other side, where Jesus originally told the disciples to go.

   i.   It's very possible that if they had stood and believed, this would have happened for them even before Jesus showed up on the scene.

B. At times, God will tell us to do things that go against the normal flow of nature.

C. God lives in the supernatural realm, and if we are truly following Him, we will too.

D. If we haven't ever been in a situation like that, where we've gotten in over our heads, it's probably because we're playing it too safe.

E. We need to step out of the boat and start walking on the water!

TEACHER'S GUIDE

1. After Jesus fed five thousand men with five loaves and two fish, look what happened:

> Jesus constrained his disciples to get into a ship, and to go before him unto the other side, *while he sent the multitudes away.* [23] *And when he had sent the multitudes away, he went up into a mountain apart to pray: and when the evening was come, he was there alone.* [24] *But the ship was now in the midst of the sea, tossed with waves: for the wind was contrary.*
>
> Matthew 14:22-24, emphasis mine

Jesus' words about going to the other side were spoken by the Creator (Col. 1:16). He is the one who spoke that very lake into existence—all of His words carried that same creative power. If the Lord has ever told us something, He meant every single bit of it. The disciples didn't think about who had told them to do this. Jesus was the parent force, and He said, "Get in and go to the other side!"—the disciples didn't understand whom they were dealing with.

1a. "*Jesus constrained his disciples to get into a ship, and to go before him _____*" (Matt. 14:22).
   A. "*And wait*"
   B. "*And swim across*"
   C. "*Unto the other side*"
   D. All of the above
   E. None of the above
   C. *"Unto the other side"*
1b. What did the disciples not understand?
   Whom they were dealing with
1c. *Discussion question:* How do you react when you don't focus on what God has told you to do?
   Discussion question

2. The disciples had glimpsed who Jesus was, but they weren't keeping it foremost in their thoughts. If they had really thought about who had told them to do this, they wouldn't have been so overwhelmed. In the midst of the storm, the disciples could have stood on the Lord's word to them and said, "He didn't tell us to go to the middle of the lake and run the risk of drowning!" They had what they needed to accomplish Jesus' instructions; they just reverted to being carnal and forgot all the supernatural lessons taught that day.

2a. Why were the disciples so overwhelmed by the storm?
   They weren't keeping Jesus foremost in their thoughts
2b. Why did the disciples revert to being carnal?
   They forgot all the supernatural lessons Jesus had taught that day
2c. *Discussion question:* How do you keep Jesus foremost in your thoughts?
   Discussion question

3. Most people would say, "You can't fault the disciples. Look, the winds were really bad!" but again, that's because they magnify physical, natural things instead of God. When the Lord spoke to the disciples, He didn't say, "Guys, I'm sorry; I shouldn't have left you out on the sea by yourself." Andrew believes the Lord expects us to do better than most of us are doing; we have His promises but just aren't believing them. Many people identify with the disciples and say, "I understand exactly how they felt; it's hard to maintain your faith when you're in the midst of a storm!" Although the Lord understands and has compassion on us, that isn't normal. It may be normal according to those who don't believe God, but it isn't the normal Christian life. We need to recognize and focus on whom we serve, the command He's given us, and what He's already done. Instead of being overcome by our problems, we can overcome our problems by His promises. If the disciples had put absolute faith in what Jesus said, they could have walked on the water.

3a. Why do most people not find fault with the disciples?
   Most magnify physical, natural things instead of God
3b. True or false: When the Lord spoke to the disciples, He said, "Guys, I'm sorry; I shouldn't have left you out on the sea by yourself."
   False
3c. Instead of being overcome by your problems, you can overcome your problems by_____.
   His promises
3d. *Discussion question:* What could happen in your life if you put absolute faith in what Jesus said?
   Discussion question

4. John's account of Jesus walking on the water shows us another important detail:

   Then they willingly received him [Jesus] into the ship: and immediately the ship was at the land whither they went.

   John 6:21, brackets mine

The boat and all its inhabitants were instantly transported to the other side, where Jesus originally told the disciples to go. It's very possible that if they had stood and believed, this would have happened for them even before Jesus showed up on the scene. At times, God will tell us to do things that go against the normal flow of nature. God lives in the supernatural realm, and if we are truly following Him, we will too. If we haven't ever been in a situation like that where we've gotten in over our heads, it's probably because we're playing it too safe. So, we need to step out of the boat and start walking on the water!

4a. True or false: It's very possible that if the disciples had stood and believed, this miracle would have happened for them even before Jesus showed up on the scene.
True

4b. God lives in the supernatural realm, and if you are truly following Him, _____.
You will too

4c. If you haven't ever been in a situation like that where you've gotten in over your head, it's probably because of what?
A. You're a great swimmer
B. You're playing it too safe
C. You're a great time manager
D. All of the above
E. None of the above
B. You're playing it too safe

4d. *Discussion question:* What does "stepping out of the boat" look like for you?
Discussion question

DISCIPLESHIP QUESTIONS

1. *"Jesus constrained his disciples to get into a ship, and to go before him
    _____"* (Matt. 14:22).
    A.   *"And wait"*
    B.   *"And swim across"*
    C.   *"Unto the other side"*
    D.   All of the above
    E.   None of the above

2. What did the disciples not understand?

    _____

    _____

    _____

3. *Discussion question:* How do you react when you don't focus on what God has
    told you to do?

    _____

    _____

    _____

4. Why were the disciples so overwhelmed by the storm?

    _____

    _____

    _____

5. Why did the disciples revert to being carnal?

    _____

    _____

    _____

6. *Discussion question:* How do you keep Jesus foremost in your thoughts?

_____

_____

_____

7. Why do most people not find fault with the disciples?

_____

_____

_____

8. True or false: When the Lord spoke to the disciples, He said, "Guys, I'm sorry; I shouldn't have left you out on the sea by yourself."

9. Instead of being overcome by your problems, you can overcome your problems by_____.

10. *Discussion question:* What could happen in your life if you put absolute faith in what Jesus said?

_____

_____

_____

11. True or false: It's very possible that if the disciples had stood and believed, this miracle would have happened for them even before Jesus showed up on the scene.

12. God lives in the supernatural realm, and if you are truly following Him, _____.

13. If you haven't ever been in a situation like that where you've gotten in over your head, it's probably because of what?
    A.   You're a great swimmer
    B.   You're playing it too safe
    C.   You're a great time manager
    D.   All of the above
    E.   None of the above

14. *Discussion question:* What does "stepping out of the boat" look like for you?

_____

_____

_____

ANSWER KEY

1. C. *"Unto the other side"*

2. Whom they were dealing with

3. *Discussion question*

4. They weren't keeping Jesus foremost in their thoughts

5. They forgot all the supernatural lessons Jesus had taught that day

6. *Discussion question*

7. Most magnify physical, natural things instead of God

8. False

9. His promises

10. *Discussion question*

11. True

12. You will too

13. B. You're playing it too safe

14. *Discussion question*

SCRIPTURES

MATTHEW 14:22-33

And straightway Jesus constrained his disciples to get into a ship, and to go before him unto the other side, while he sent the multitudes away. [23] And when he had sent the multitudes away, he went up into a mountain apart to pray: and when the evening was come, he was there alone. [24] But the ship was now in the midst of the sea, tossed with waves: for the wind was contrary. [25] And in the fourth watch of the night Jesus went unto them, walking on the sea. [26] And when the disciples saw him walking on the sea, they were troubled, saying, It is a spirit; and they cried out for fear. [27] But straightway Jesus spake unto them, saying, Be of good cheer; it is I; be not afraid. [28] And Peter answered him and said, Lord, if it be thou, bid me come unto thee on the water. [29] And he said, Come. And when Peter was come down out of the ship, he walked on the water, to go to Jesus. [30] But when he saw the wind boisterous, he was afraid; and beginning to sink, he cried, saying, Lord, save me. [31] And immediately Jesus stretched forth his hand, and caught him, and said unto him, O thou of little faith, wherefore didst thou doubt? [32] And when they were come into the ship, the wind ceased. [33] Then they that were in the ship came and worshipped him, saying, Of a truth thou art the Son of God.

COLOSSIANS 1:16-17

For by him were all things created, that are in heaven, and that are in earth, visible and invisible, whether they be thrones, or dominions, or principalities, or powers: all things were created by him, and for him: [17] And he is before all things, and by him all things consist.

JOHN 1:1

In the beginning was the Word, and the Word was with God, and the Word was God.

JOHN 1:3

All things were made by him; and without him was not any thing made that was made.

HEBREWS 1:3

Who being the brightness of his glory, and the express image of his person, and upholding all things by the word of his power, when he had by himself purged our sins, sat down on the right hand of the Majesty on high.

MATTHEW 16:16

And Simon Peter answered and said, Thou art the Christ, the Son of the living God.

MARK 6:45-52

And straightway he constrained his disciples to get into the ship, and to go to the other side before unto Bethsaida, while he sent away the people. [46] And when he had sent them away, he departed into a mountain to pray. [47] And when even was come, the ship was in the midst of the sea, and he alone on the land. [48] And he saw them toiling in rowing; for the wind was contrary unto them: and about the fourth watch of the night he cometh unto them, walking upon the sea, and would have passed by them. [49] But when they saw him walking upon the sea, they supposed it had been a spirit, and cried out: [50] For they all saw him, and were troubled. And immediately he talked with them, and saith unto them, Be of good cheer: it is I; be not afraid. [51] And he went up unto them into the ship; and the wind ceased: and they were sore amazed in themselves beyond measure, and wondered. [52] For they considered not the miracle of the loaves: for their heart was hardened.

MARK 4:39

And he arose, and rebuked the wind, and said unto the sea, Peace, be still. And the wind ceased, and there was a great calm.

1 JOHN 5:4

For whatsoever is born of God overcometh the world: and this is the victory that overcometh the world, even our faith.

JOHN 6:15-21

When Jesus therefore perceived that they would come and take him by force, to make him a king, he departed again into a mountain himself alone. [16] And when even was now come, his disciples went down unto the sea, [17] And entered into a ship, and went over the sea toward Capernaum. And it was now dark, and Jesus was not come to them. [18] And the sea arose by reason of a great wind that blew. [19] So when they had rowed about five and twenty or thirty furlongs, they see Jesus walking on the sea, and drawing nigh unto the ship: and they were afraid. [20] But he saith unto them, It is I; be not afraid. [21] Then they willingly received him into the ship: and immediately the ship was at the land whither they went.

HE WOULD HAVE PASSED THEM BY

LESSON 2

And in the fourth watch of the night Jesus went unto them, walking on the sea. [26] And when the disciples saw him walking on the sea, they were troubled, saying, It is a spirit; and they cried out for fear.

Matthew 14:25-26

Notice how Mark records this:

And he saw them toiling in rowing; for the wind was contrary unto them: and about the fourth watch of the night he cometh unto them, walking upon the sea, and would have passed by them.

Mark 6:48

Jesus was praying on a mountain overlooking the Sea of Galilee. He was in the same storm, so He knew what was going on. It's not like He was indifferent to the disciples' needs. The Lord knew exactly what they were going through, because He was going through it too. He was 100 percent aware of their problem!

It's reasonable to guess that Jesus came down and started walking on the water so He could rescue His disciples. But even though He drew near to help them, He made as though He *"would have passed by them"* (Mark 6:48). In other words, even though it seems clear that the Lord came to the disciples' rescue, presented Himself, and even came close enough for them to see Him, the Scriptures say that He would have passed them by.

Think about that! It seems obvious that He was coming to help them. Yet He didn't just run out there, wave His arms, and yell, "Guys, don't panic! It's Me! Here I am to save the day!" The Lord revealed Himself to them, but it was their responsibility to call out to Him by faith and to reach out and make a demand on His miracle-working power. He revealed Himself to them, but they should have tapped into what He had on the inside of Him to be able to receive this miracle.

The disciples' responsibility to respond in faith to Jesus' presence is a perfect parallel to how God provides miracles for us today. It doesn't matter what our situations are—God knows what we're going through, and He's touched with the same feelings. Jesus is present with us in our circumstances. Responding in faith to His presence is our part.

GOD KNOWS

When Saul saw the Lord on the road to Damascus, Jesus cried out to him, saying,

> *Saul, Saul, why persecutest thou me?*
>
> Acts 9:4

Saul had never personally persecuted the Lord Jesus Christ when He walked the earth in His physical body. Rather, he was persecuting the post-Resurrection followers of Jesus. This shows us how personally our Lord takes things. Whatever we do to a member of the body of Christ, we do to Him.

> *Inasmuch as ye have done* it *unto one of the least of these my brethren, ye have done* it *unto me.*
>
> Matthew 25:40, emphasis mine

The Lord knows what you're going through. He knows your situation—every feeling, every hurt, every need. At times you may think, *Nobody knows the trouble I have,* and you feel as though you have to explain it to God. Yet the Word says,

> *Your Father knoweth what things ye have need of, before ye ask him.*
>
> Matthew 6:8

"COME BOLDLY!"

The Lord has already been touched with the feeling of your infirmities. He knows exactly what you're going through and will reveal Himself to you (Heb. 4:15). He never leaves you nor forsakes you (Heb. 13:5). God is with you to deliver you from whatever situation you're in. But just as He appeared to His disciples and would have passed them by, you have to make a demand on His power. It's up to you to *"come boldly unto the throne of grace, that* [you] *may obtain mercy, and find grace to help in time of need"* (Heb. 4:16, brackets mine).

Crying out in desperation and pity, saying, "God, don't You love me? Where are You? Do You exist? Do You care?" isn't making a demand on God. If anything, that's tying His hands, because you're doubting His Word. You're doubting His promise that He'll never leave you nor forsake you (Heb. 13:5).

If the disciples were thinking they were going to die, then they were doubting God's Word. Jesus told them to get into the boat and go over to the other side. He didn't say, "Get into the boat and drown trying to get to the other side." They doubted His Word. They weren't aware of how powerful the promise was that He had given them.

We can only speculate about why the disciples didn't call out to Jesus in faith. It seems that He intervened on their behalf without any response of faith on their part. The Word says that He *"would have passed by them"* (Mark 6:48). It's possible they could've died if the Lord hadn't intervened and rescued them.

PEOPLE MAKE CHOICES

People who adhere to an extreme "sovereignty of God" type of teaching really get upset with this truth. They say, "Nothing can happen but what God wills or allows. He orchestrates everything perfectly according to His plan." Wrong! God's Word abounds with examples that contradict this false assumption.

God wills *"above all things that thou mayest prosper and be in health, even as thy soul prospereth"* (3 John 2). Yet people suffer poverty and die all the time of sickness and disease.

Also, the Lord is *"not willing that any should perish, but that* all *should come to repentance"* (2 Pet. 3:9, emphasis mine). However, Jesus Himself said that many would perish through the broad gate leading to destruction and few would enter by the narrow gate to everlasting life (Matt. 7:13-14). God's will does not automatically come to pass. What He *wants* and what He *wills* can be thwarted.

Now, don't get confused about this. I'm talking about God's will for an individual's life. God is so wise and awesome that if Satan blocks His overall plan one way, the Lord will find some other person to work through and eventually get His will accomplished another way. I don't doubt that at all! But on an individual basis, people die without it being the Lord's will. It's His will for them to be healed, but, for one reason or another, they don't receive the healing He's already provided. God doesn't will for wars, heartache, tragedy, divorce, etc., to occur. He's not the one who makes those things happen. People make choices.

BELIEVE GOD

Jesus revealed Himself to the disciples. He was there and His power was available. Because they didn't respond to Him positively and draw on His supernatural ability in one way or another, it's possible they could have drowned.

You may be in a crisis situation and needing God to do something right away. You may be begging and pleading, but if you don't reach out in faith, you might drown. You need to respond positively to God's Word so that it comes alive and stands up on the inside of you. If you don't believe God, He might just pass on by. It's not automatic that you win. You must believe God!

ANDREW'S RECOMMENDATIONS FOR FURTHER STUDY

For a more in-depth look at this, please refer to my teachings titled "The Sovereignty of God," "God's Not Guilty," and *Spiritual Authority*.

OUTLINE

I.   Jesus was in the same storm, so He knew what was going on with His disciples:

And he saw them toiling in rowing; for the wind was contrary unto
them: and about the fourth watch of the night he cometh unto them,
walking upon the sea, and would have passed by them.

Mark 6:48

A. Even though it seems clear that the Lord came to the disciples' rescue, presented Himself, and even came close enough for them to see Him, the Scriptures say that He would have passed them by.

B. The Lord revealed Himself to them, but it was their responsibility to call out to Him by faith and to reach out and make a demand on His miracle-working power.

C. The disciples' responsibility to respond in faith to Jesus' presence is a perfect parallel to how God provides miracles for us today.

II. It doesn't matter what our situations are—God knows what we're going through, and He's touched with the same feelings.

A. For example, Saul had never personally persecuted the Lord Jesus Christ when He walked the earth in His physical body, but Jesus cried out to him, saying,

Saul, Saul, why persecutest thou me?

Acts 9:4

   i.   Saul (Paul) was persecuting the post-Resurrection followers of Jesus.

B. This shows us how personally our Lord takes things.

C. Whatever we do to a member of the body of Christ, we do to Him.

Inasmuch as ye have done it unto one of the least of these my brethren,
ye have done it unto me.
Matthew 25:40, emphasis mine

D. At times we may think, *Nobody knows the trouble I have,* yet the Word says,

Your Father knoweth what things ye have need of, before ye ask him.
Matthew 6:8

III. The Lord knows exactly what you're going through (Heb. 4:15).

   A. God is with you to deliver you from whatever situation you're in.

   B. But just as He appeared to His disciples and would have passed them by, it's up to you to *"come boldly unto the throne of grace, that* [you] *may obtain mercy, and find grace to help in time of need"* (Heb. 4:16, brackets mine).

   C. Crying out in desperation and pity, saying, "God, don't You love me? Where are You? Do You exist? Do You care?" isn't making a demand on God.

   D. If anything, you're doubting His promise that He'll never leave you nor forsake you (Heb. 13:5).

IV. Jesus didn't say, "Get into the boat and drown trying to get to the other side."

   A. They doubted His Word because they weren't aware of how powerful the promise was that He had given them.

   B. We can only speculate about why the disciples didn't call out to Jesus in faith.

   C. It seems that He intervened on their behalf without any response of faith on their part.

   D. It's possible they could've died if the Lord hadn't intervened and rescued them.

V. People who adhere to an extreme "sovereignty of God" type of teaching really get upset with the truth that Jesus would have passed them by.

   A. They say, "Nothing can happen but what God wills or allows. He orchestrates everything perfectly according to His plan."

   B. God's Word abounds with examples that contradict this false assumption.

   C. God wills *"above all things that thou mayest prosper and be in health, even as thy soul prospereth"* (3 John 2), yet people suffer poverty and die all the time of sickness and disease.

   D. Also, the Lord is *"not willing that any should perish, but that* all *should come to repentance"* (2 Pet. 3:9, emphasis mine); however, Jesus Himself said that many would perish through the broad gate leading to destruction and few would enter by the narrow gate to everlasting life (Matt. 7:13-14).

VI. What God *wants* and what He *wills* can be thwarted.

    A. God is so wise and awesome that if Satan blocks His overall plan one way, the Lord will find some other person to work through and eventually get His will accomplished another way.

    B. But on an individual basis, people die without it being the Lord's will.

    C. God doesn't will for wars, heartache, tragedy, divorce, etc., to occur.

    D. People make choices.

VII. You may be in a crisis situation and needing God to do something right away.

    A. You may be begging and pleading, but if you don't reach out in faith, you might drown.

    B. You need to respond positively to God's Word so that it comes alive and stands up on the inside of you.

    C. If you don't believe God, He might just pass on by.

    D. It's not automatic that you win.

ANDREW'S RECOMMENDATIONS FOR FURTHER STUDY

For a more in-depth look at this, please refer to my teachings titled "The Sovereignty of God," "God's Not Guilty," and *Spiritual Authority*.

Teacher's Guide

1. Jesus was in the same storm, so He knew what was going on with His disciples:

> *And he saw them toiling in rowing; for the wind was contrary unto them: and about the fourth watch of the night he cometh unto them, walking upon the sea, and would have passed by them.*
>
> Mark 6:48

Even though it seems clear that the Lord came to the disciples' rescue, presented Himself, and even came close enough for them to see Him, the Scriptures say that He would have passed them by. The Lord revealed Himself to them, but it was their responsibility to call out to Him by faith and to reach out and make a demand on His miracle-working power. The disciples' responsibility to respond in faith to Jesus' presence is a perfect parallel to how God provides miracles for us today.

1a. True or false: Because Jesus was in the same storm, He knew what was happening with the disciples.
   True
1b. When Jesus revealed Himself to them, what was it their responsibility to do?
   Call out to Him by faith and make a demand on His power
1c. *Discussion question:* Why do you have to respond in faith to Jesus' presence in order to receive His miracle-working power?
   Discussion question

2. It doesn't matter what our situations are—God knows what we're going through and He's touched with the same feelings. For example, Saul had never personally persecuted the Lord Jesus Christ when He walked the earth in His physical body, but Jesus cried out to him, saying,

> *Saul, Saul, why persecutest thou me?*
>
> Acts 9:4

Saul (Paul) was persecuting the post-Resurrection followers of Jesus. This shows us how personally our Lord takes things. Whatever we do to a member of the body of Christ, we do to Him.

> *Inasmuch as ye have done* it *unto one of the least of these my brethren, ye have done* it *unto me.*
>
> Matthew 25:40, emphasis mine

At times we may think, *Nobody knows the trouble I have,* yet the Word says,

> *Your Father knoweth what things ye have need of, before ye ask him.*
>
> Matthew 6:8

2a. It doesn't matter what your _____ is; God knows what you're going through and He's _____ with the same feelings.
    <u>Situation / touched</u>

2b. True or false: Jesus cried out to Saul (Paul) *"Saul, Saul, why persecutest thou me?"* because he was persecuting Jesus when He walked on the earth.
    <u>False</u>

2c. Jesus told Paul that he was persecuting Him because of what?
    A. Paul was persecuting the post-Resurrection followers of Jesus
    B. The Lord took His followers' deaths personally
    C. Whatever you do to a member of Christ's body, you do to Him
    D. All of the above
    E. None of the above
    <u>D. All of the above</u>

2d. *Discussion question:* Why is it *always* untrue for anyone to say, "Nobody knows the trouble I have"?
    <u>*Discussion question*</u>

3. The Lord knows exactly what we're going through (Heb. 4:15). God is with us to deliver us from whatever situations we're in. But just as He appeared to His disciples and would have passed them by, it's up to us to *"come boldly unto the throne of grace, that [you] may obtain mercy, and find grace to help in time of need"* (Heb. 4:16, brackets mine). Crying out in desperation and pity, saying, "God, don't You love me? Where are You? Do You exist? Do You care?" isn't making a demand on God. If anything, we're doubting His promise that He'll never leave us nor forsake us (Heb. 13:5).

3a. God is always with you and ready to do what for you?
    <u>Deliver you from any situation you are in</u>

3b. *Discussion question:* Why is it up to you if Jesus delivers you or just passes you by?
    <u>*Discussion question*</u>

3c. Which of the following prayers makes a demand of faith on God?
    A. "God, don't You love me?"
    B. "God, where are You? Don't You care?"
    C. "God, I know I can come boldly to Your throne and find grace in time of need"
    D. All of the above
    E. None of the above
    <u>C. "God, I know I can come boldly to Your throne and find grace in time of need"</u>

4. Jesus didn't say, "Get into the boat and drown trying to get to the other side." They doubted His Word because they weren't aware of how powerful the promise was that He had given them. We can only speculate about why the disciples didn't call out to Jesus in faith. It seems that He intervened on their behalf without any response of faith on their part. It's possible they could've died if the Lord hadn't intervened and rescued them.

4a. What caused the disciples to doubt Jesus' word that they would get to the other side?
    A. They thought they were going to drown
    B. They weren't aware of how powerful the promise was that He had given them
    C. Jesus told them that the best He could do was to try to get them to the other side
    D. All of the above
    E. None of the above
    B. They weren't aware of how powerful the promise was that He had given them

4b. *Discussion question:* Describe a time in your life when you believe you could have seriously suffered, or even died, if the Lord hadn't intervened on your behalf.
    Discussion question

5. People who adhere to an extreme "sovereignty of God" type of teaching really get upset with the truth that Jesus would have passed them by. They say, "Nothing can happen but what God wills or allows. He orchestrates everything perfectly according to His plan." God's Word abounds with examples that contradict this false assumption. God wills *"above all things that thou mayest prosper and be in health, even as thy soul prospereth"* (3 John 2), yet people suffer poverty and die all the time of sickness and disease. Also, the Lord is *"not willing that any should perish, but that all should come to repentance"* (2 Pet. 3:9, emphasis mine); however, Jesus Himself said that many would perish through the broad gate leading to destruction and few would enter by the narrow gate to everlasting life (Matt. 7:13-14).

5a. *Discussion question:* Since it's always God's will that people prosper and be in health, even as their souls prosper (3 John 2), why do people still suffer poverty and die all the time from sickness and disease?
    Discussion question

6. What God *wants* and what He *wills* can be thwarted. God is so wise and awesome that if Satan blocks His overall plan one way, the Lord will find some other person to work through and eventually get His will accomplished another way. But on an individual basis, people die without it being the Lord's will. God doesn't will for wars, heartache, tragedy, divorce, etc., to occur. People make choices.

6a. True or false: Individuals may thwart God's will for their lives, but God's overall plan for humanity cannot be blocked or thwarted.
True

6b. If Satan blocks God's plan one way, the Lord will find some _____ _____ to work through to get His will accomplished.
Other person

6c. What causes war, heartache, tragedy, divorce, etc., to occur?
People make choices

7. We may be in a crisis situation and needing God to do something right away. We may be begging and pleading, but if we don't reach out in faith, we might drown. We need to respond positively to God's Word so that it comes alive and stands up on the inside of us. If we don't believe God, He might just pass on by. It's not automatic that we win.

7a. *Discussion question:* Based on this lesson, what do believers have to do so that God is able to respond and help them in a crisis (or any) situation?
Discussion question

DISCIPLESHIP QUESTIONS

1. True or false: Because Jesus was in the same storm, He knew what was happening with the disciples.

2. When Jesus revealed Himself to them, what was it their responsibility to do?

    _____

    _____

    _____

3. *Discussion question:* Why do you have to respond in faith to Jesus' presence in order to receive His miracle-working power?

    _____

    _____

    _____

4. It doesn't matter what your _____ is; God knows what you're going through and He's _____ with the same feelings.

5. True or false: Jesus cried out to Saul (Paul) "Saul, Saul, why persecutest thou me?" because he was persecuting Jesus when He walked on the earth.

6. Jesus told Paul that he was persecuting Him because of what?
    A. Paul was persecuting the post-Resurrection followers of Jesus
    B. The Lord took His followers' deaths personally
    C. Whatever you do to a member of Christ's body, you do to Him
    D. All of the above
    E. None of the above

7. *Discussion question:* Why is it always untrue for anyone to say, "Nobody knows the trouble I have"?

    _____

    _____

    _____

8.   God is always with you and ready to do what for you?

      _____

      _____

      _____

9.   *Discussion question:* Why is it up to you if Jesus delivers you or just passes you by?

      _____

      _____

      _____

10.   Which of the following prayers makes a demand of faith on God?
      A.   "God, don't You love me?"
      B.   "God, where are You? Don't You care?"
      C.   "God, I know I can come boldly to Your throne and find grace in time of need"
      D.   All of the above
      E.   None of the above

11.   What caused the disciples to doubt Jesus' word that they would get to the other side?
      A.   They thought they were going to drown
      B.   They weren't aware of how powerful the promise was that He had given them
      C.   Jesus told them that the best He could do was to try to get them to the other side
      D.   All of the above
      E.   None of the above

12.   *Discussion question:* Describe a time in your life when you believe you could have seriously suffered, or even died, if the Lord hadn't intervened on your behalf.

      _____

      _____

      _____

13. *Discussion question:* Since it's always God's will that people prosper and be in health, even as their souls prosper (3 John 2), why do people still suffer poverty and die all the time from sickness and disease?

_____

_____

_____

14. True or false: Individuals may thwart God's will for their lives, but God's overall plan for humanity cannot be blocked or thwarted.

15. If Satan blocks God's plan one way, the Lord will find some _____ _____ to work through to get His will accomplished.

16. What causes war, heartache, tragedy, divorce, etc., to occur?

_____

_____

_____

17. *Discussion question:* Based on this lesson, what do believers have to do so that God is able to respond and help them in a crisis (or any) situation?

_____

_____

_____

ANSWER KEY

1. True

2. Call out to Him by faith and make a demand on His power

3. *Discussion question*

4. Situation / touched

5. False

6. D. All of the above

7. *Discussion question*

8. Deliver you from any situation you are in

9. *Discussion question*

10. C. "God, I know I can come boldly to Your throne and find grace in time of need"

11. B. They weren't aware of how powerful the promise was that He had given them

12. *Discussion question*

13. *Discussion question*

14. True

15. Other person

16. People make choices

17. *Discussion question*

Scriptures

MATTHEW 14:25-26

And in the fourth watch of the night Jesus went unto them, walking on the sea. [26] And when the disciples saw him walking on the sea, they were troubled, saying, It is a spirit; and they cried out for fear.

MARK 6:48

And he saw them toiling in rowing; for the wind was contrary unto them: and about the fourth watch of the night he cometh unto them, walking upon the sea, and would have passed by them.

ACTS 9:4

Saul, Saul, why persecutest thou me?

MATTHEW 25:40

And the King shall answer and say unto them, Verily I say unto you, Inasmuch as ye have done it unto one of the least of these my brethren, ye have done it unto me.

MATTHEW 6:8

Be not ye therefore like unto them: for your Father knoweth what things ye have need of, before ye ask him.

HEBREWS 4:15-16

For we have not an high priest which cannot be touched with the feeling of our infirmities; but was in all points tempted like as we are, yet without sin. [16] Let us therefore come boldly unto the throne of grace, that we may obtain mercy, and find grace to help in time of need.

HEBREWS 13:5

Let your conversation be without covetousness; and be content with such things as ye have: for he hath said, I will never leave thee, nor forsake thee.

3 JOHN 2

Beloved, I wish above all things that thou mayest prosper and be in health, even as thy soul prospereth.

2 PETER 3:9

The Lord is not slack concerning his promise, as some men count slackness; but is longsuffering to us-ward, not willing that any should perish, but that all should come to repentance.

BE OF GOOD CHEER

LESSON 3

But when they saw him walking upon the sea, they supposed it had been a spirit, and cried out.

Mark 6:49

The disciples couldn't believe that Jesus was walking on top of the very thing that was about to destroy them. Jesus was so cool and so in control.

When we're overwhelmed by the storm, it can cause us to miss the Lord and not draw on His supernatural ability. We can't believe that the very thing that is overwhelming us is nothing to God. We miss the fact that He can walk on top of the very problem that's about to drown us. Many times we're looking for the Lord to be as worried and upset as we are. We think He's going to wring His hands and say, "This is a really big problem!" But that's never going to be the response of the Lord!

Some people say, "Oh, we need to pray! We need lots of people to fast and pray together. It's going to take two, three, or four hundred people on the prayer chain praying, because this is such a big deal! If God provides this miracle, all the lights of heaven are liable to dim. I'm not sure that He can actually pull this off!" They may not use this terminology, but they're expressing the same concept. They think God is as overwhelmed as they are.

Jesus is walking on top of the water—the very thing that's overwhelming you. Whatever your situation is, it's no problem for the Lord. Really, it's no big deal!

NO PROBLEM FOR JESUS

The only thing that makes something a big deal is our unbelief. We tend to magnify how terrible our situation is. However, it would do us good just to look at things from God's perspective and realize that it's no big deal.

Jesus was walking on top of the very thing that was raging around the disciples, and they supposed it had been a spirit (Mark 6:49). In other words, they just couldn't believe that this wasn't bothering God. They couldn't believe that He wasn't struggling the same way they were. The disciples were probably thinking, *Surely, this is some kind of vision coming toward us. It can't be real—Jesus can't walk on top of water. This is not normal. It's not natural!*

God isn't limited by the physical realm the way we are. Yet many times we really do think He is. I've been asked, "Have you ever heard of anybody being healed of AIDS? I've heard of cancers being healed, but not AIDS." Nothing—absolutely nothing—is impossible with God! Of course He can handle AIDS! But we think a million dollars, five million dollars, a house payment, a car payment—whatever it is— is just too big, even for God. We expect Him to feel like, "Hey, I just can't pull this off in such short notice. I need more time to do it." God isn't like that. He can walk on top of anything that's about to destroy us. We need to get used to God being supernatural!

Everyone struggles with this. Sometimes we live so much in the natural realm that it just seems like, "God, is there really a way out of this?" There's always a way out— nothing is too difficult for God. Whatever our problem is, Jesus is on top of it. He's not under it. He's not sinking. He's on top of it. It's no problem for Jesus!

BOTHERED?

For they all saw him, and were troubled. And immediately he talked with them, and saith unto them, Be of good cheer: it is I; be not afraid.

Mark 6:50

This verse shows just how completely in control God is. The things that are bothering you aren't bothering God. And if you appropriate what is yours in Christ, you won't need to be bothered either. You really won't! Why? Jesus said,

Be of good cheer: it is I; be not afraid.

Mark 6:50b

The Lord was speaking to people who were concerned that they might drown. They knew they could be up to their necks in water in no time. Those guys were sailors. They were not men who were easily frightened. It wasn't because they were afraid and fearful about something that wasn't truly a serious situation. In the midst of the crisis, Jesus told them, "Be of good cheer. It's Me. Don't be afraid!"

SAME STUFF—DIFFERENT WRAPPER

You might be in a situation right now where you think that there's just no way to really rejoice until you see absolute deliverance. However, you can get to a place right there in the midst of it where you're of good cheer. "But, Andrew, you haven't been where I am!" Although I probably haven't been in your identical situation, the Bible says,

> *There hath no temptation taken you but such as is common to man.*
>
> 1 Corinthians 10:13

If you think that your situation is unique, you're wrong. If you are exempting yourself from the encouragement I'm trying to give you because you think your situation is worse than mine, then you're exempting yourself from the very answers you need to overcome it. No situation has taken you except what is *common* to man.

I get the same stuff—it just comes wrapped in a different package with a different bow! But I've proven in my life over and over again that you can rejoice when there is no reason to do so in the natural. You can rejoice when there's no rationale, no proof, no evidence of anything—except your faith!

"YOU'RE A GOOD GOD!"

In the early part of March 2001, my wife and I had just returned home from an international flight. We didn't get to bed until sometime around midnight. Then, at 4:15 in the morning, I received a call from my oldest son, saying, "Dad, I'm sorry to tell you this, but Peter [my youngest son] is dead." He told me what happened and I said, "Don't let anyone touch him until I get there. The first report is not the last report!"

I told my wife what I had just heard, and we prayed. We commanded life to come back into Peter. Then we jumped out of bed and got dressed. It took about an hour and fifteen minutes to drive from our house to the hospital in Colorado Springs.

On the drive in, I didn't know what was going to happen. I had prayed, spoken, and was believing God for a miracle. I knew the Lord had more for my younger son than what he had experienced. He wasn't living in the fullness of God. I knew there was more for him, but at the same time, there are things people can do that short-circuit the plan of God for their lives. So, I didn't know what was going to happen.

After Jamie and I prayed, we didn't say very much because we didn't want to speak forth doubt and unbelief. But finally I couldn't stand it any longer. Unbelief, sorrow, and grief were beginning to get hold of me. So, as we were driving in, I just started saying, "God, You're a good God!" Just like the Lord said in Mark 6:50, I started cheering myself up and speaking against fear, saying, "Father, You're a good God. I want You to know that whether Peter lives or not, You are a good God. You didn't do this. You didn't cause it." And I just went to praising Him.

As I did, I started remembering prophecies that the Lord had given me about my children—things that hadn't happened yet. The Bible says that we can war a good warfare by the prophecies that have gone before (1 Tim. 1:18). So, I thought, *Father, if You prophesied this, then he has to live.* So, I just started praising God, and by the time we arrived in Colorado Springs, I was excited and happy. I was expecting something wonderful to happen!

FAITH REJOICES BEFORE

Peter had been dead for about five hours and had already turned black, but when I walked into the room, my oldest son said, "Dad, within five or ten minutes after I called you, Peter just sat up!" They'd already put a toe tag on him. He was stripped naked and put in a cooler. They'd already pronounced him dead and gone—but he sat up!

I talked to the nurse about it and asked him twice if Peter was actually dead. He told me, "Nobody comes in here like that and leaves alive."

"So, was he dead?"

"If this ever happens again, he'll leave in a body bag!"

I suspect that for liability reasons, they wouldn't say Peter had died. I don't have a medical certificate to "prove" that my son was dead, but he'd already turned black and hadn't breathed for five hours. I believe God raised him from the dead. However, before that situation had resolved, I was praising God and full of good cheer!

You might be in the same position the disciples were in when the Lord told them to be of good cheer. The storm was still raging. The boat may have even been sinking. It looked like they might drown. Everything was still at its worst, but Jesus said, "Be of good cheer. It's Me. Don't be afraid!"

Most people can't be of good cheer unless they see their physical problems resolve. Then, when everything works out, they'll be of good cheer. But faith doesn't work that way. We must first get into faith, resist fear, and be of good cheer while the storm is still raging and the ship is going down. Then, afterwards is when we see the miracle. Think about that. If all the Lord wanted was for His disciples to be of good cheer, He could have stilled the storm first, and then their joy would have come. But He told them to be of good cheer before He stilled the storm. That's because He was probably trying to solicit a response of faith from them. He's seeking the same thing from us today.

Anyone can be of good cheer and overcome fear once the storm stops and the boat is translated to the other side, but it takes faith to rejoice before you know what the outcome will be!

OUTLINE

I.   When we're overwhelmed by the storm, it can cause us to miss the Lord.

But when they saw him walking upon the sea, they supposed it had been a spirit, and cried out.

Mark 6:49

A. We can't believe that the very thing that is overwhelming us is nothing to God.

B. Many times, we're looking for the Lord to be as worried and upset as we are, saying, "If God provides this miracle, all the lights of heaven are liable to dim."

C. Jesus is walking on top of the water—the very thing that's overwhelming us.

II. The only thing that makes something a big deal is our unbelief.

A. We tend to magnify how terrible our situation is; however, it would do us good just to look at things from God's perspective and realize that it's no big deal.

B. The disciples were probably thinking, *Surely this is some kind of vision coming toward us; it can't be real—Jesus can't walk on top of water.*

C. God isn't limited by the physical realm the way we are.

D. Sometimes we live so much in the natural realm that it just seems like, "God, is there really a way out of this?" but nothing is too difficult for God.

E. Whatever our problem is, Jesus is on top of it—

For they all saw him, and were troubled. And immediately he talked with them, and saith unto them, Be of good cheer: it is I; be not afraid.

Mark 6:50

F. The things that are bothering us aren't bothering God.

G. And if we appropriate what is ours in Christ, we won't need to be bothered either.

III. You might be in a situation right now where you think that there's just no way to really rejoice until you see absolute deliverance.

   A. However, you can get to a place in the midst of it where you're of good cheer—

   There hath no temptation taken you but such as is common to man.
                                                                    1 Corinthians 10:13

   B. If you think that your situation is unique, you're exempting yourself from the answers you need to overcome it.

   C. I've proven in my life over and over that you can rejoice when there is no reason—except faith.

IV. Most people can't be of good cheer unless they see their physical problems resolve.

   A. But faith doesn't work that way; you must first get into faith, resist fear, and be of good cheer while the storm is still raging and the ship is going down.

   B. Jesus told the disciples to be of good cheer before He stilled the storm.

   C. Anyone can be of good cheer and overcome fear once the storm stops and the boat is translated to the other side, but it takes faith to rejoice before you know what the outcome will be!

TEACHER'S GUIDE

1. When we're overwhelmed by the storm, it can cause us to miss the Lord:

> *But when they saw him walking upon the sea, they supposed it had been a spirit, and cried out.*
>
> Mark 6:49

We can't believe that the very thing that is overwhelming us is nothing to God. Many times, we're looking for the Lord to be as worried and upset as we are, saying, "If God provides this miracle, all the lights of heaven are liable to dim." Jesus is walking on top of the water—the very thing that's overwhelming us.

1a. True or false: When you're overwhelmed by the storm, it can cause you to miss the Lord.
   True

1b. You can't believe that the very thing that is overwhelming you is _____ to God.
   A. Overwhelming
   B. Nothing
   C. Good
   D. Stressful
   E. Destructive
   B. Nothing

1c. *Discussion question:* Why do you think it's sometimes difficult to see Jesus walking on top of life's problems?
   Discussion question

2. The only thing that makes something a big deal is our unbelief. We tend to magnify how terrible our situation is; however, it would do us good just to look at things from God's perspective and realize that it's no big deal. The disciples were probably thinking, *Surely this is some kind of vision coming toward us; it can't be real—Jesus can't walk on top of water.* God isn't limited by the physical realm the way we are. Sometimes we live so much in the natural realm that it just seems like, "God, is there really a way out of this?" but nothing is too difficult for God. Whatever our problem is, Jesus is on top of it—

> *For they all saw him, and were troubled. And immediately he talked with them, and saith unto them, Be of good cheer: it is I; be not afraid.*
>
> Mark 6:50

The things that are bothering us aren't bothering God. And if we appropriate what is ours in Christ, we won't need to be bothered either.

2a. What is the only thing that makes something a big deal?
  Your unbelief
2b. True or false: God is limited by the physical realm the way you are.
  False
2c. *Discussion question:* Since God isn't bothered by your problems, how do you think God would handle a problem you've had or are currently going through?
  Discussion question

3. We might be in a situation right now where we think that there's just no way to really rejoice until we see absolute deliverance. However, we can get to a place in the midst of it where we're of good cheer—

> *There hath no temptation taken you but such as is common to man.*
> 1 Corinthians 10:13

If we think that our situation is unique, we're exempting ourselves from the answers we need to overcome it. Andrew has proven in his life over and over that we can rejoice when there is no reason—except faith.

3a. Many people think there is no way to really rejoice until what?
  They see absolute deliverance
3b. True or false: You have to wait until a problem is solved to rejoice.
  False
3c. What are people doing when they say that their situation is unique?
  Exempting themselves from the answers they need to overcome it
3d. *Discussion question:* What are other ways you exempt yourself from solutions?
  Discussion question

4. Most people can't be of good cheer unless they see their physical problems resolve. But faith doesn't work that way; we must first get into faith, resist fear, and be of good cheer while the storm is still raging and the ship is going down. Jesus told the disciples to be of good cheer before He stilled the storm. Anyone can be of good cheer and overcome fear once the storm stops and the boat is translated to the other side, but it takes faith to rejoice before you know what the outcome will be!

4a. How does faith work in a problem?
  Faith resists fear and is of good cheer while the storm is raging

4b. Jesus told the disciples to be of good cheer _____ He stilled the storm.

    A. While

    B. After

    C. When

    D. If

    E. Before

    E. Before

4c. True or false: It takes faith to rejoice after you know the outcome.

    False

4d. *Discussion question:* What are other ways you can exercise your faith in a storm?

    Discussion question

DISCIPLESHIP QUESTIONS

1. True or false: When you're overwhelmed by the storm, it can cause you to miss the Lord.

2. You can't believe that the very thing that is overwhelming you is _____ to God.
    A.   Overwhelming
    B.   Nothing
    C.   Good
    D.   Stressful
    E.   Destructive

3. *Discussion question:* Why do you think it's sometimes difficult to see Jesus walking on top of life's problems?

    _____

    _____

    _____

4. What is the only thing that makes something a big deal?

    _____

    _____

    _____

5. True or false: God is limited by the physical realm the way you are.

6. *Discussion question:* Since God isn't bothered by your problems, how do you think God would handle a problem you've had or are currently going through?

    _____

    _____

    _____

7. Many people think there is no way to really rejoice until what?

_____

_____

_____

8. True or false: You have to wait until a problem is solved to rejoice.

9. What are people doing when they say that their situation is unique?

_____

_____

_____

10. *Discussion question:* What are other ways you exempt yourself from solutions?

_____

_____

_____

11. How does faith work in a problem?

_____

_____

_____

12. Jesus told the disciples to be of good cheer _____ He stilled the storm.
    A. While
    B. After
    C. When
    D. If
    E. Before

13. True or false: It takes faith to rejoice after you know the outcome.

14.   *Discussion question:* What are other ways you can exercise your faith in a storm?

_____

_____

_____

ANSWER KEY

1. True

2. B. Nothing

3. *Discussion question*

4. Your unbelief

5. False

6. *Discussion question*

7. They see absolute deliverance

8. False

9. Exempting themselves from the answers they need to overcome it

10. *Discussion question*

11. Faith resists fear and is of good cheer while the storm is raging

12. E. Before

13. False

14. *Discussion question*

SCRIPTURES

MARK 6:49-50

But when they saw him walking upon the sea, they supposed it had been a spirit, and cried out. [50] For they all saw him, and were troubled. And immediately he talked with them, and saith unto them, Be of good cheer: it is I; be not afraid.

1 CORINTHIANS 10:13

There hath no temptation taken you but such as is common to man: but God is faithful, who will not suffer you to be tempted above that ye are able; but will with the temptation also make a way to escape, that ye may be able to bear it.

1 TIMOTHY 1:18

This charge I commit unto thee, son Timothy, according to the prophecies which went before on thee, that thou by them mightest war a good warfare.

DON'T BE AFRAID

LESSON 4

Are you in the midst of a storm in your life? Is your boat filling up with water fast? Do you feel like you're about to drown? If so, then Jesus is saying to you now,

Be of good cheer: it is I; be not afraid.

Mark 6:50

If you genuinely understand this truth, it's enough to make you shout! The Word of God will come alive and make you stand up on the inside, and if you stand up on the inside, eventually you'll stand up on the outside too. That's when you'll see your physical circumstances change. That's when you'll walk on the water!

SYMPATHY OR FAITH?

I once was talking with a man at church with whom I'd been praying for healing. Although he saw some improvement in his physical body, the main issue was that he had been discouraged and hurt in his attitude and emotions. After listening to my messages over and over again, he finally started to get it. He told me, "I really believe that if I can ever get myself encouraged and stand up on the inside, then I'll stand up on the outside."

I responded, "That's it!"

He was getting a glimpse of it. He wasn't there yet, but he could see it. He was pressing forward in that direction, and it was just a matter of time before he would see the physical manifestation. Why? Because he was being of good cheer. He was overcoming fear while the storm was still raging.

Most people would criticize us for encouraging a cancer patient by saying, "Be of good cheer. Don't be afraid. The Lord is with you! Why don't you praise God right now for your healing?" They'd say, "Don't you understand the pain this person is going through? The doctor says they're going to die, and here you are speaking 'faith.'

You're showing no sympathy whatsoever!" They don't understand that once they are calm on the inside, it's just a matter of time before things become calm on the outside. Once we receive the answer in our hearts, it will manifest itself in the physical realm.

The traditional approach to dealing with people's problems in the church today, however, is to join people in their pity by saying, "You are absolutely justified in being angry, bitter, and hurt. I know those feelings too!" We just get down, wallow, cry, and get as discouraged and defeated as they are in an effort to "comfort" them. Basically, we're trying to sympathize with them. I'm not saying that we should be insensitive, unloving, or refuse to acknowledge that someone is struggling. But we need to give them something beyond that.

We need to do what Jesus did. Most people today would say, "Jesus was insensitive. How could He tell people who were in one of the worst storms of their lives and possibly facing drowning, *'Be of good cheer: it is I; be not afraid'*? That's unreasonable." But Jesus was a "faith" person. There's no doubt about it! People might criticize Him for it, but we need more people like that. We really do.

"IT'S NO BIG DEAL!"

A young woman in our church who had just gotten married went around telling everyone that she wanted a dozen kids. Some people questioned the wisdom of that, but it was her choice. That's what she wanted. She just couldn't wait to become pregnant and have children.

Her husband was a minister, and they would itinerate up to six months at a time. One time while she and her husband were ministering at a church, word came back that she was pregnant. We rejoiced because we all knew how much she wanted children. However, when they returned, she went to the doctor and found out it was a tubular pregnancy. Instead of her having a child, the doctor discovered she had cancer and said, "If I don't remove all of your female organs through an operation, you'll be dead within a week. Even with the surgery, you only have a fifty-fifty chance of living. And if you do live, you'll never be able to have children."

She was given a bleak prognosis. At best, her number one goal of being a mother of twelve looked out of reach. Although I'd heard about her prognosis from someone, I was busy laughing, joking, and cutting up after a midweek service, when she came up and tapped me on the shoulder. I turned around, and through tears, she blubbered, "Andrew, have they told you what happened to me?"

I couldn't turn off my joy and excitement just because of her situation, so I looked right at her and declared, "Cancer is no problem with God! You act like this is a big deal. It's no big deal!"

I might as well have slapped her in the face. She stopped crying, looked at me, and asked, "What are you saying?"

I said, "It's not any harder for God to heal cancer than it is for Him to heal a cold. You could just believe God. You don't have to go without children, and you don't have to die in a week's time."

She asked if Jamie and I would come over and talk to her and her husband about this, so we did. I simply told them, "This is only a big thing because you've made it big. It's not hard for God. It's not like it's going to make the lights in heaven dim if you ask the Lord to heal you."

She asked, "So, should I continue to go to the doctor? Should I have the surgery?"

"Well, that's up to you. It's your choice. It's not sin if you do, but if they take out all of your female organs, you aren't going to have any children. There was only one virgin birth, and you aren't going to have another. That's not the way it works. If it were me, I'd just believe God!"

"But they told me I'd be dead in a week!"

"Well, if you believe that, then you need to let them do the operation. There's nothing wrong with that. If that is where your faith is, go for it. But you can believe God. It's not a problem for Him!"

She chose to believe God. Although it's a long story, it's been at least fifteen years and four or five children ago since all that happened. She lived, and she had all her kids through natural childbirth because any doctor who saw her records wouldn't believe she could have a normal delivery. So, she just had all her babies at home. It wasn't a problem!

"THIS IS GOING TO BE SOME AWESOME MIRACLE!"

It's not wrong to show compassion toward people who are hurting, but we must go beyond that. We also need to show faith and give encouragement to people. It wouldn't have done any good if Jesus had gone out there and said, "Guys, it's terrible. I can't believe what's happening to you. This is big, really big!" He was the only hope the disciples had. If He had magnified the problem, expressed unbelief, and talked about how bad things were for them, they would have been in big trouble. Jesus needed to minimize the situation, magnify God, and show that His power was so much greater than their circumstances. He did that by walking on top of the very thing that had the potential to destroy them, saying, in effect, "Guys, don't be afraid.

Be of good cheer. You ought to be happy, because you're about to see one awesome miracle!" When our faith is quickened, we will get excited and say, "God, this is going to be one awesome miracle!"

My faith quickened while I was driving into Colorado Springs the morning my son died. After hearing the report, I prayed and started praising God. All of a sudden, faith rose up and I began to get excited. Part of what I was thinking was, *God, this is going to be some awesome miracle. He's already been dead for five hours, turned black, and is not breathing. Boy, this is going to be some great miracle!* And it was! But before I actually saw it, I was excited about what God was going to do.

That's what Jesus was telling the disciples when He said, "Be of good cheer!" They could have actually been excited earlier and said, "Jesus told us to go to the other side—not to drown. Yet there is no way in the natural that we're getting to the other side. This is going to be some awesome miracle!"

TRANSLATED

John's account reveals how they were translated to the other side of the lake.

And immediately the ship was at the land whither they went.

John 6:21

BOOM! They covered approximately two miles, and there they were! Instantly the wind ceased, and there was a great calm. Most of us would be thrilled, saying, "Wow, that's awesome! Wouldn't it have been wonderful to have been there?" In a sense, that's what Jesus was saying. It hadn't happened yet. The disciples were in the middle of the storm, but the Lord knew they weren't going to drown in the middle of the lake. He knew it was going to work out, so He basically said, "Guys, rejoice! You ought to get a load of this. You're about to experience one awesome demonstration of My power!"

This sounds totally off-the-wall to many people, because they live so much in the natural that they don't ever get to a place where they rejoice in the midst of a trying situation. Other folks have heard enough teaching on this that they might rejoice through gritted teeth as "warfare," but not from a genuine heart of faith. They're trying to obtain victory rather than merely enforce it.

That's okay if that's where you are spiritually. There's a time and place for doing it that way. But after a while, you get to the point when you've seen so many victories that you're not just rejoicing through gritted teeth. It's not just something you're forcing yourself to do. You can actually get to a place where you genuinely rejoice because you just know that something awesome is going to come out of your situation!

MIDNIGHT PRAISE

And at midnight Paul and Silas prayed, and sang praises unto God: and the prisoners heard them. [26] And suddenly there was a great earthquake, so that the foundations of the prison were shaken: and immediately all the doors were opened, and every one's bands were loosed. [27] And the keeper of the prison awaking out of his sleep, and seeing the prison doors open, he drew out his sword, and would have killed himself, supposing that the prisoners had been fled. [28] But Paul cried with a loud voice, saying, Do thyself no harm: for we are all here.

Acts 16:25-28

Paul and Silas were in the Philippian jail. They didn't just pray and sing praises at midnight so that they could be delivered. That wasn't why they were singing and praising God. How do I know? When the Lord sent the earthquake, all the prison doors opened and every man's shackles fell off his feet, but Paul and Silas didn't leave. They just kept right on praising.

If praising God to get deliverance had been their motive, they would have left as soon as the prison doors opened. But they were actually praising God out of a pure heart of love. They were excited and worshiping the Lord for who He is. They had actually moved into the place that Jesus was talking about. They were of good cheer and not afraid.

Paul and Silas were rejoicing in their relationship with God. They knew He would take care of things, so they just rejoiced. When deliverance came, they didn't even take it. They stayed in jail. And not just Paul and Silas—every one of the unsaved prisoners stayed too. Wow! For all of those ungodly people to stay in their prison cells even after they'd been loosed was the result of one powerful manifestation of the presence of God.

EITHER WAY, YOU WIN!

You can get to a place where you really are of good cheer and not afraid—even while the storms of life are raging around you. It's not just something you're trying to accomplish; you're there. You have good cheer even in the midst of your situation.

If the doctor tells you that you're going to die, just go to praising God and say, "Father, this is awesome! It would be wonderful if I went to be with You!"

We sing songs like "When we all get to heaven," but then when the doctor tells us that we're going there, we start crying. Did we really mean what we sang? If we think about this properly, we'd recognize that if we die, we get to go be with the Lord, and if we receive our healing—which Jesus has already provided for us—then we'll have an awesome testimony. Either way, we win!

If you could get your healing to manifest, it would become a great testimony. It could even open up your entire ministry. You could travel the world, telling about how awesome God is for this healing. But if you don't see healing manifest, you get to go be with Him. You could be of good cheer and not afraid, regardless of your situation and its outcome. Praise the Lord!

ANDREW'S RECOMMENDATIONS FOR FURTHER STUDY

For additional encouragement concerning how to manifest your healing, please refer to my teachings titled *God Wants You Well*, *How to Receive a Miracle*, and *You've Already Got It!*

OUTLINE

I. If you're in the midst of a storm and your boat is filling up with water fast, Jesus is saying to you,

> *Be of good cheer: it is I; be not afraid.*
>
> Mark 6:50

A. If you genuinely understand this truth, it's enough to make you shout!

B. The Word of God will come alive and make you stand up on the inside, and if you stand up on the inside, eventually you'll stand up on the outside too.

C. That's when you'll see your physical circumstances change, and you'll walk on the water.

D. Being of good cheer is overcoming fear while the storm is still raging.

II. Most people would criticize us for encouraging a cancer patient by saying, "Be of good cheer."

A. They'd say, "Don't you understand the pain this person is going through? The doctor says they're going to die and here you are speaking 'faith.' You're showing no sympathy whatsoever!"

B. They don't understand that once they are calm on the inside, it's just a matter of time before things become calm on the outside.

C. The traditional approach to dealing with people's problems in the church today is to join people in their pity—basically, we're trying to sympathize with them.

D. I'm not saying that we should be insensitive, unloving, or refuse to acknowledge that someone is struggling.

E. But we need to do what Jesus did—He told people who were in one of the worst storms of their lives and possibly facing drowning, *Be of good cheer: it is I; be not afraid"* (Mark 6:50).

III. It's not wrong to show compassion toward people who are hurting, but we must go beyond that to show faith and give encouragement to people.

A. It wouldn't have done any good if Jesus had gone out there and said, "Guys, it's terrible. I can't believe what's happening to you. This is big, really big!"

B. He was the only hope the disciples had, so if He had magnified the problem, expressed unbelief, and talked about how bad things were for them, they would have been in big trouble.

C. Jesus needed to minimize the situation, magnify God, and show that His power was so much greater than their circumstances.

D. He did that by walking on top of the very thing that had the potential to destroy them, saying, in effect, "Guys, don't be afraid. Be of good cheer. You ought to be happy, because you're about to see one awesome miracle!"

E. When our faith is quickened, we will get excited and say, "God, this is going to be one awesome miracle!"

IV. In a sense, what Jesus meant when He said "Be of good cheer" was that although the disciples were still in a storm, they could rejoice because they were about to experience an awesome demonstration of God's power.

A. Many people live so much in the natural that they don't ever get to a place where they rejoice in the midst of a trying situation.

B. Other folks have heard enough teaching on this that they might rejoice through gritted teeth as "warfare," but not from a genuine heart of faith.

C. You can actually get to a place where you genuinely rejoice because you just know that something awesome is going to come out of your situation, which is how Paul and Silas were in the Philippian jail (Acts 16:25-28).

V. Paul and Silas didn't just pray and sing praises at midnight so that they could be delivered.

A. We know this because when the Lord sent the earthquake, all the prison doors opened and every man's shackles fell off his feet, but Paul and Silas didn't leave; they just kept right on praising.

B. If praising God to get deliverance had been their motive, they would have left just as soon as the prison doors opened.

C. But they were actually praising God out of a pure heart of love.

D. They were excited and worshiping the Lord for who He is.

E. They had actually moved into the place that Jesus was talking about and were of good cheer and not afraid.

F. Paul and Silas were rejoicing in their relationship with God, so when deliverance came, they stayed in jail, and every one of those unsaved prisoners stayed too!

G. For all of those ungodly people to stay in their prison cells even after they'd been loosed was the result of one powerful manifestation of the presence of God.

VI. You can get to a place where you really are of good cheer and not afraid—even while the storms of life are raging around you.

A. It's not just something you're trying to accomplish; you're there.

B. If the doctor tells you that you're going to die, just go to praising God and say, "Father, this is awesome! It would be wonderful if I went to be with You!"

   i. You sing songs like "When we all get to heaven," but then when the doctor tells you that you're going there, you start crying.

   ii. Did you really mean what you sang?

C. If you think about this properly, you'd recognize that if you die, you get to go be with the Lord, and if you receive your healing—which Jesus has already provided for you—then you'll have an awesome testimony.

D. It could even open up your entire ministry.

   i. You could travel the world, telling about how awesome God is for this healing.

   ii. But if you don't see healing manifest, you get to go be with Him.

E. You could be of good cheer and not afraid, regardless of your situation and its outcome.

ANDREW'S RECOMMENDATIONS FOR FURTHER STUDY

For additional encouragement concerning how to manifest your healing, please refer to my teachings titled *God Wants You Well*, *How to Receive a Miracle*, and *You've Already Got It!*

TEACHER'S GUIDE

1. If we're in the midst of a storm and our boat is filling up with water fast, Jesus is saying to us,

> *Be of good cheer: it is I; be not afraid.*
>
> Mark 6:50

If we genuinely understand this truth, it's enough to make us shout! The Word of God will come alive and make us stand up on the inside, and if we stand up on the inside, eventually we'll stand up on the outside too. That's when we'll see our physical circumstances change, and we'll walk on the water. Being of good cheer is overcoming fear while the storm is still raging.

1a. What would Jesus tell you when He finds you in the midst of a raging storm?
   A. "Be of good cheer"
   B. "You're on your own"
   C. "Prepare for the next life"
   D. All of the above
   E. None of the above
   A. "Be of good cheer"
1b. What needs to come alive on the inside of you for you to stand up on the inside?
   The Word
1c. While the storm is still raging, being of good cheer is overcoming _____.
   Fear

2. Most people would criticize us for encouraging a cancer patient by saying, "Be of good cheer." They'd say, "Don't you understand the pain this person is going through? The doctor says they're going to die and here you are speaking 'faith.' You're showing no sympathy whatsoever!" They don't understand that once they are calm on the inside, it's just a matter of time before things become calm on the outside. The traditional approach to dealing with people's problems in the church today is to join people in their pity—basically, we're trying to sympathize with them. Andrew is not saying that we should be insensitive, unloving, or refuse to acknowledge that someone is struggling. But we need to do what Jesus did—He told people who were in one of the worst storms of their lives and possibly facing drowning, *Be of good cheer: it is I; be not afraid"* (Mark 6:50).

2a. True or false: It is common to tell a sick person to be of good cheer.
   False

2b. In the church, the traditional way of dealing with people in crisis is to do what?
   A. Encourage them
   B. Sympathize with their problems
   C. Ignore them
   D. All of the above
   E. None of the above
   B. Sympathize with their problems
2c. Instead of sympathizing with people's problems, you need to do what
   _____ did and tell people to be of good cheer and not be _____ .
   Jesus / afraid

3. It's not wrong to show compassion toward people who are hurting, but we must go beyond that to show faith and give encouragement to people. It wouldn't have done any good if Jesus had gone out there and said, "Guys, it's terrible. I can't believe what's happening to you. This is big, really big!" He was the only hope the disciples had, so if He had magnified the problem, expressed unbelief, and talked about how bad things were for them, they would have been in big trouble. Jesus needed to minimize the situation, magnify God, and show that His power was so much greater than their circumstances. He did that by walking on top of the very thing that had the potential to destroy them, saying, in effect, "Guys, don't be afraid. Be of good cheer. You ought to be happy because you're about to see one awesome miracle!" When our faith is quickened, we will get excited and say, "God, this is going to be one awesome miracle!"

3a. More than showing hurting people compassion, what must you show and give them?
   Faith and encouragement
3b. What did Jesus do when He spoke to His disciples?
   A. Magnified their problems
   B. Expressed unbelief
   C. Talked about how bad things were for them
   D. All of the above
   E. None of the above
   E. None of the above
3c. Jesus _____ the situation and _____ God.
   Minimized / magnified

4. In a sense, what Jesus meant when He said "Be of good cheer" was that although the disciples were still in a storm, they could rejoice because they were about to experience an awesome demonstration of God's power. Many people live so much in the natural that they don't ever get to a place where they rejoice in the midst of a trying situation. Other folks have heard enough teaching on this that they might rejoice through gritted teeth as "warfare," but not from a genuine heart of faith. We

can actually get to a place where we genuinely rejoice because we just know that something awesome is going to come out of our situation, which is how Paul and Silas were in the Philippian jail (Acts 16:25-28).

4a. Many people live so much in the natural that they never get to a place where they _____ in the midst of a trying situation.

Rejoice

4b. People who have had enough teaching about being of good cheer may rejoice, but it's through _____ _____.

Gritted teeth

4c. *Discussion question:* How have you handled storms in your own life, and what did you learn?

Discussion question

5. Paul and Silas didn't just pray and sing praises at midnight so that they could be delivered. We know this because when the Lord sent the earthquake, all the prison doors opened and every man's shackles fell off his feet, but Paul and Silas didn't leave; they just kept right on praising. If praising God to get deliverance had been their motive, they would have left just as soon as the prison doors opened. But they were actually praising God out of a pure heart of love. They were excited and worshiping the Lord for who He is. They had actually moved into the place that Jesus was talking about and were of good cheer and not afraid. Paul and Silas were rejoicing in their relationship with God, so when deliverance came, they stayed in jail, and every one of those unsaved prisoners stayed too! For all of those ungodly people to stay in their prison cells even after they'd been loosed was the result of one powerful manifestation of the presence of God

5a. Why did Paul and Silas stay in their jail cells, praising the Lord, when the earthquake opened the prison doors?

They were praising God out of a pure heart, not just to be delivered

5b. True or false: Paul and Silas were excited and worshiping God for who He was to them.

True

5c. *Discussion question:* How have you experienced the power of God?

Discussion question

6. We can get to a place where we really are of good cheer and not afraid—even while the storms of life are raging around us. It's not just something we're trying to accomplish, but we're there. If the doctor tells us that we're going to die, then we can just go to praising God and say, "Father, this is awesome! It would be wonderful if I went to be with You!" We sing songs like "When we all get to heaven," but then when

the doctor tells us that we're going there, we start crying. Did we really mean what we sang? If we think about this properly, we'd recognize that if we die, we get to go be with the Lord, and if we receive our healing—which Jesus has already provided for us—then we'll have an awesome testimony. It could even open up our entire ministry. We could travel the world, telling about how awesome God is for this healing. But if we don't see healing manifest, we get to go be with Him. We could be of good cheer and not afraid, regardless of our situation and its outcome.

6a. *Discussion question:* How do you think you can get to a place where you really are of good cheer, even when the storms of life are raging around you?
   Discussion question

6b. If the doctor says you're going to die, you will either die and go to _____ with the Lord, or the Lord will heal you and you will have an awesome _____.
   Be / testimony

6c. Regardless of the outcome of your situation, what can you do?
   Be of good cheer and not be afraid

DISCIPLESHIP QUESTIONS

1. What would Jesus tell you when He finds you in the midst of a raging storm?
    A. "Be of good cheer"
    B. "You're on your own"
    C. "Prepare for the next life"
    D. All of the above
    E. None of the above

2. What needs to come alive on the inside of you for you to stand up on the inside?

    _____

    _____

    _____

3. While the storm is still raging, being of good cheer is overcoming _____.

4. True or false: It is common to tell a sick person to be of good cheer.

5. In the church, the traditional way of dealing with people in crisis is to do what?
    A. Encourage them
    B. Sympathize with their problems
    C. Ignore them
    D. All of the above
    E. None of the above

6. Instead of sympathizing with people's problems, you need to do what
    _____ did and tell people to be of good cheer and not be _____.

7. More than showing hurting people compassion, what must you show and give them?

    _____

    _____

    _____

8. What did Jesus do when He spoke to His disciples?
   A. Magnified their problems
   B. Expressed unbelief
   C. Talked about how bad things were for them
   D. All of the above
   E. None of the above

9. Jesus _____ the situation and _____ God.

10. Many people live so much in the natural that they never get to a place where they _____ in the midst of a trying situation.

11. People who have had enough teaching about being of good cheer may rejoice, but it's through _____ _____.

12. *Discussion question:* How have you handled storms in your own life, and what did you learn?

   _____

   _____

   _____

13. Why did Paul and Silas stay in their jail cells, praising the Lord, when the earthquake opened the prison doors?

   _____

   _____

   _____

14. True or false: Paul and Silas were excited and worshiping God for who He was to them.

15. *Discussion question:* How have you experienced the power of God?

   _____

   _____

   _____

16. *Discussion question:* How do you think you can get to a place where you really are of good cheer, even when the storms of life are raging around you?

_____

_____

_____

17. If the doctor says you're going to die, you will either die and go to _____ with the Lord, or the Lord will heal you and you will have an awesome _____.

18. Regardless of the outcome of your situation, what can you do?

_____

_____

_____

ANSWER KEY

1. A. "Be of good cheer"

2. The Word

3. Fear

4. False

5. B. Sympathize with their problems

6. Jesus / afraid

7. Faith and encouragement

8. E. None of the above

9. Minimized / magnified

10. Rejoice

11. Gritted teeth

12. *Discussion question*

13. They were praising God out of a pure heart, not just to be delivered

14. True

15. *Discussion question*

16. *Discussion question*

17. Be / testimony

18. Be of good cheer and not be afraid

SCRIPTURES

MARK 6:50

For they all saw him, and were troubled. And immediately he talked with them, and saith unto them, Be of good cheer: it is I; be not afraid.

JOHN 6:21

Then they willingly received him into the ship: and immediately the ship was at the land whither they went.

ACTS 16:25-28

And at midnight Paul and Silas prayed, and sang praises unto God: and the prisoners heard them. [26] And suddenly there was a great earthquake, so that the foundations of the prison were shaken: and immediately all the doors were opened, and every one's bands were loosed. [27] And the keeper of the prison awaking out of his sleep, and seeing the prison doors open, he drew out his sword, and would have killed himself, supposing that the prisoners had been fled. [28] But Paul cried with a loud voice, saying, Do thyself no harm: for we all are here.

A Word from God

If you don't exhibit faith while the storm is still raging, there's a possibility you won't see your deliverance. Many people go through the motions, praising God and saying some of the right things, but they're just wishing and hoping that it's going to work; they aren't really believing. When you truly start believing, you'll find yourself abounding in thanksgiving.

> As ye have therefore received Christ Jesus the Lord, so walk ye in him:
> [7] Rooted and built up in him, and stablished in the faith, as ye have
> been taught, abounding therein with thanksgiving.
>
> Colossians 2:6-7

The way faith abounds is through thanksgiving. If you don't have a thankful heart, if you aren't being of good cheer in the midst of your storm, it's possible that you may have faith, but your faith isn't abounding—overcoming—greater than your fears. When you really get into a God kind of faith, you'll find that you can persist to the point of excitement and joy. I'm not talking about something you manufacture yourself. It comes from God. It's a calm assurance, a peace, and a joy that comes from knowing that God is faithful. He's never forsaken you, and He never will.

Before the Lord performed the miracle the disciples needed, He essentially told them, "Trust Me. Be of good cheer. It's Me. Don't be afraid. Don't you remember who I am? I'm the one who just fed the multitude. I miraculously multiplied a tiny bit of food. I'm the one who has already seen the dead raised, blind eyes and deaf ears opened, and demons cast out. It's Me! Don't you realize who you're serving? Don't you recognize who's with you? It's Me!"

You need to recognize who Jesus is on the inside of you. Once you do this, you will not be afraid. You will experience His joy and peace, and you will be of good cheer!

"GET IN AND GO!"

Everything we've discussed thus far is essential before stepping out onto the water. We need to have a word from God. The disciples had a command from the Lord Jesus

Christ. They didn't embark out onto the sea on their own. It wasn't their will to go across then and there. It was His.

> *And straightway Jesus constrained his disciples to get into a ship, and to go before him unto the other side.*
>
> Matthew 14:22

"Constrained" means that Jesus had to use some force. He didn't physically grab his disciples and throw them into the boat. However, they did express some type of resistance to getting into the ship and going across at that time, so Jesus constrained them. He basically told them, "Get in and go!"

Why did the disciples resist? Why did Jesus have to constrain them? Many of them had grown up as fishermen on the Sea of Galilee. This body of water is famous for having storms come down over the mountains north and east of it. Those mountains would hide storms until they crested over the tops. Then the storms would quickly rush down upon the sea. Due to this, it was important to be in tune with what the weather was like.

THE WEATHER REPORT

Most of us don't understand this because we discern what the weather is like by listening to a weatherman. We have virtually no weather sense whatsoever. I remember pastoring a little group of ranchers in Pritchett, Colorado, and they would say, "Well, it's going to rain tonight."

I'd ask, "Did you hear that on the weather report?"

They'd say, "No." They just felt the barometric pressure changing and the humidity in the air. Sure enough, it would be exactly as they thought. They'd say, "Boy, that wind is coming out of the north. That means we're going to have a 'northerner' come in." Those guys were much better than the weatherman at predicting the weather. After being around them for just a short period of time, I began picking those things up too. I was soon able to tell when a winter storm was coming in.

The disciples were far more in tune with the weather than we are today. That's why Jesus had to constrain them. That storm may not have hit yet, but they could see it coming. All the signs were there, and it was against their better judgment to be out on the Sea of Galilee at that time. Yet they went because Jesus told them to.

ENCOUNTERING ADVERSITY IN GOD'S WILL

In Matthew 14, Jesus' disciples had a word from God. But that didn't mean they weren't going to have any problems. Remember, the winds were contrary, and the disciples were struggling to get to the other side; yet they were perfectly in the center of God's will. They voiced their reservations, but the Lord—knowing full well what they were feeling—essentially said, "No, go to the other side. It'll work!"

You can be perfectly led by God and still experience hardship. Satan will come against you. There will be circumstances in your life that will make it seem as though you're not going to make it, but that isn't always an indication that you have missed God.

The disciples were doing exactly what the Lord told them to do. He was aware of their situation and was there to help them. However, He didn't just step in and deliver them. He wanted them to cooperate. He wanted them to call out to Him in faith.

It's important for you to discern in your own situation whether the adversity you're suffering is the result of your own ignorance or disobedience. For instance, Jonah ran away from God. Instead of following the Lord's instructions, he got into a storm that almost cost him his life. But that storm was totally out of God's will. It was something he shouldn't have had to experience.

You need to be honest enough to evaluate where you are. Is the situation, the storm, or the struggle you're in the result of your own rebellion toward God, as it was in the case of Jonah? Did you or did you not have a word from Him when you left the shore? Did the Lord tell you to move in a specific direction at this time?

PAUL AND SILAS

Paul and Silas encountered great adversity while in the center of God's will.

> *And a vision appeared to Paul in the night; There stood a man of Macedonia, and prayed him, saying, Come over into Macedonia, and help us. [10] And after he had seen the vision, immediately we endeavoured to go into Macedonia, assuredly gathering that the Lord had called us for to preach the gospel unto them.*
>
> Acts 16:9-10

Within just a few days of being in Philippi (a city in Macedonia province), Paul and Silas were beaten and thrown in jail (Acts 16:22-24). Following God doesn't mean that your life is going to be storm-less, jail-less, or problem-less. Although many people teach that if it is God's will, everything will just work out perfectly—that's just not true.

On another occasion, Paul wrote,

> *For a great door and effectual is opened unto me, and there are many adversaries.*
>
> 1 Corinthians 16:9

God led Paul into Philippi, where he was thrown into prison within a short period of time. Just because you're in a storm and it looks like you're about to drown doesn't mean that you've missed God. Don't let circumstances dictate God's will!

CALL OUT TO GOD

Did you have a word from God or not? If so, stand on it, being full of good cheer, because He is with you. Don't be afraid. Exhibit faith before you see the final outcome. Faith is seeing the miracle manifest in your heart before you see it manifest in the physical realm. Start praising, worshiping, and rejoicing before you win your battle. Anyone can praise God after everything is taken care of, but it's a Bible principle that you must operate in faith before you see the physical manifestation.

Regardless of your problem, the Lord is there with you. He knows your situation just as surely as He knew the circumstances the disciples were in. He went out there to help them, but He wanted them to cry out to Him in faith. You need to call out to God. Don't just sit there in silence and let your problems overtake you. Call out to God!

Don't call out in unbelief like the disciples did when Jesus was walking on the water toward them and they thought He was ghost or something. Don't cry out in frustration, anger, or bitterness. Call out to Him in faith. Make a demand. Draw on the power of God that is available to you. Express your faith and be of good courage. Don't be afraid. Remember who it is you are serving. Let your faith abound in thanksgiving. When you do these things out of a heart of faith, you're laying the groundwork for the miracle God is about to perform on your behalf.

If you are in a situation that looks as if it will overcome you, take courage. Start believing God. Make sure that you've heard from Him and are in the center of His will. Then call out to God in faith and make a demand on Him and His power. Start rejoicing and be of good cheer, even before you see the storm stilled!

OVERCOME!

Once you're truly in faith, you can have such a good time in Him that whether your circumstances ever work out or not isn't the issue. You believe God and possess the proof—faith in your heart. You'll want it to work out for other people's benefit as much as or more than your own. You'll just want it to be a great testimony to encourage others and bring glory to God!

The Lord loves you and wants you to be a water walker. He desires that you overcome the storms of life instead of being overcome by them. These simple-yet-powerful truths will help you do just that!

Outline

I. Many people go through the motions, praising God and saying some of the right things, but they're just wishing and hoping that it's going to work.

   A. When you truly start believing, you'll find yourself abounding in thanksgiving—

> *As ye have therefore received Christ Jesus the Lord, so walk ye in him:* [7] *Rooted and built up in him, and stablished in the faith, as ye have been taught, abounding therein with thanksgiving.*
>
> Colossians 2:6-7

   B. The way faith abounds is through thanksgiving.

   C. When you really get into a God kind of faith, you'll find that you can persist to the point of excitement and joy.

   D. You need to recognize who Jesus is on the inside of you; once you do this, you will experience His joy and peace and be of good cheer!

II. The disciples voiced their reservations, but the Lord—knowing full well what they were feeling—essentially said, "No, go to the other side. It'll work!"

   A. They were doing exactly what the Lord told them to do.

   B. It's important for you to discern in your own situation whether the adversity you're suffering is the result of your own ignorance or disobedience.

   C. Instead of following the Lord's instructions, Jonah got into a storm that almost cost him his life.

      i. But that storm was totally out of God's will; it was something he shouldn't have had to experience.

   D. You need to evaluate where you are; did you or did you not have a word from God to move in a specific direction?

III. Paul and Silas encountered great adversity while in the center of God's will—

> *And a vision appeared to Paul in the night; There stood a man of Macedonia, and prayed him, saying, Come over into Macedonia, and help us. [10] And after he had seen the vision, immediately we endeavoured to go into Macedonia, assuredly gathering that the Lord had called us for to preach the gospel unto them.*
>
> Acts 16:9-10

    A. Within just a few days of being in Philippi, Paul and Silas were beaten and thrown in jail (Acts 16:22-24).

    B. Following God doesn't mean that your life is going to be storm-less, jail-less, or problem-less.

    C. Although many people teach that if it's God's will, everything will just work out perfectly—that's just not true.

        i. Paul wrote,

> *For a great door and effectual is opened unto me, and there are many adversaries.*
>
> 1 Corinthians 16:9

    D. Just because you're in a storm and it looks like you're about to drown doesn't mean that you've missed God.

IV. If you are in a situation that looks as if it will overcome you, take courage.

    A. Start believing God.

    B. Make sure that you've heard from Him and are in the center of His will.

    C. Call out to God in faith and make a demand on Him and His power.

    D. Start rejoicing and be of good cheer, even before you see the storm stilled!

TEACHER'S GUIDE

1. Many people go through the motions, praising God and saying some of the right things, but they're just wishing and hoping that it's going to work. When we truly start believing, we'll find ourselves abounding in thanksgiving—

> *As ye have therefore received Christ Jesus the Lord, so walk ye in him:*
> *[7] Rooted and built up in him, and stablished in the faith, as ye have*
> *been taught, abounding therein with thanksgiving.*
>
> Colossians 2:6-7

The way faith abounds is through thanksgiving. When we really get into a God kind of faith, we'll find that we can persist to the point of excitement and joy. We need to recognize who Jesus is on the inside of us; once we do this, we will experience His joy and peace and be of good cheer!

1a. What is a sign that you have truly started believing?
   <u>**You'll find yourself abounding in thanksgiving**</u>
1b. Faith abounds through _____.
   A. Excitement
   B. Joy
   C. Thanksgiving
   D. Courage
   E. Wishing
   <u>**C. Thanksgiving**</u>
1c. True or false: The God kind of faith persists to the point of excitement and joy.
   <u>**True**</u>
1d. When you recognize who Jesus is on the inside of you, you will what?
   <u>**Experience His joy and peace and be of good cheer**</u>

2. The disciples voiced their reservations, but the Lord—knowing full well what they were feeling—essentially said, "No, go to the other side; it'll work!" They were doing exactly what the Lord told them to do. It's important for us to discern in our own situation whether the adversity we're suffering is the result of our own ignorance or disobedience. Instead of following the Lord's instructions, Jonah got into a storm that almost cost him his life. But that storm was totally out of God's will; it was something he shouldn't have had to experience. We need to evaluate where we are; did we or did we not have a word from God to move in a specific direction?

2a. True or false: The Lord—knowing full well what the disciples were feeling—essentially said, "No, go to the other side; it'll work!"
True

2b. How do you know that the disciples were in the center of God's will during the storm?
They were doing exactly what the Lord told them to do

2c. Why was Jonah's storm totally out of God's will?
He didn't follow the Lord's instructions and got into a storm

2d. *Discussion question:* How can you be confident that you're in God's will?
Discussion question

3. Paul and Silas encountered great adversity while in the center of God's will—

> *And a vision appeared to Paul in the night; There stood a man of Macedonia, and prayed him, saying, Come over into Macedonia, and help us. [10] And after he had seen the vision, immediately we endeavoured to go into Macedonia, assuredly gathering that the Lord had called us for to preach the gospel unto them.*
>
> Acts 16:9-10

Within just a few days of being in Philippi, Paul and Silas were beaten and thrown in jail (Acts 16:22-24). Following God doesn't mean that our lives are going to be storm-less, jail-less, or problem-less. Although many people teach that if it's God's will, everything will just work out perfectly—that's not true. Paul wrote,

> *For a great door and effectual is opened unto me, and there are many adversaries.*
>
> 1 Corinthians 16:9

Just because we're in a storm and it looks like we're about to drown doesn't mean that we've missed God.

3a. True or false: Paul and Silas encountered great ease in the center of God's will.
False

3b. What happened to Paul and Silas within just a few days of being in Philippi?
They were beaten and thrown in jail

3c. True or false: If it's God's will, everything will just work out perfectly.
False

3d. *Discussion question:* How can you know you have heard from God?
Discussion question

4. If we are in a situation that looks as if it will overcome us, we should take courage, start believing God, make sure that we've heard from Him and are in the center of His will, call out to God in faith and make a demand on Him and His power, start rejoicing, and be of good cheer, even before we see the storm stilled!

4a. What should you do if you are in a storm?
   A. Be afraid
   B. Eat pizza
   C. Take a nap
   D. Take a walk
   E. Take courage
   E. Take courage

4b. What should you make sure of in a storm?
   That you've heard from Him and are in the center of His will

4c. *Discussion question:* What does it look like to take courage?
   Discussion question

4d. *Discussion question:* How can you start believing God?
   Discussion question

DISCIPLESHIP QUESTIONS

1. What is a sign that you have truly started believing?

    _____

    _____

    _____

2. Faith abounds through _____.
    A. Excitement
    B. Joy
    C. Thanksgiving
    D. Courage
    E. Wishing

3. True or false: The God kind of faith persists to the point of excitement and joy.

4. When you recognize who Jesus is on the inside of you, you will what?

    _____

    _____

    _____

5. True or false: The Lord—knowing full well what the disciples were feeling—essentially said, "No, go to the other side; it'll work!"

6. How do you know that the disciples were in the center of God's will during the storm?

    _____

    _____

    _____

7. Why was Jonah's storm totally out of God's will?

    _____

    _____

    _____

8. *Discussion question:* How can you be confident that you're in God's will?

    _____

    _____

    _____

9. True or false: Paul and Silas encountered great ease while in the center of God's will.

10. What happened to Paul and Silas within just a few days of being in Philippi?

    _____

    _____

    _____

11. True or false: If it's God's will, everything will just work out perfectly.

12. *Discussion question:* How can you know that you have heard from God?

    _____

    _____

    _____

13. What should you do if you are in a storm?
    A. Be afraid
    B. Eat pizza
    C. Take a nap
    D. Take a walk
    E. Take courage

14. What should you make sure of in a storm?

    _____

    _____

    _____

15. *Discussion question:* What does it look like to take courage?

_____

_____

_____

16. *Discussion question:* How can you start believing God?

_____

_____

_____

ANSWER KEY

1. You'll find yourself abounding in thanksgiving

2. C. Thanksgiving

3. True

4. Experience His joy and peace and be of good cheer

5. True

6. They were doing exactly what the Lord told them to do

7. He didn't follow the Lord's instructions and got into a storm

8. *Discussion question*

9. False

10. They were beaten and thrown in jail

11. False

12. *Discussion question*

13. E. Take courage

14. That you've heard from Him and are in the center of His will

15. *Discussion question*

16. *Discussion question*

Scriptures

COLOSSIANS 2:6-7

As ye have therefore received Christ Jesus the Lord, so walk ye in him:
[7] Rooted and built up in him, and stablished in the faith, as ye have
been taught, abounding therein with thanksgiving.

MATTHEW 14:22

And straightway Jesus constrained his disciples to get into a ship, and to
go before him unto the other side, while he sent the multitudes away.

ACTS 16:9-10

And a vision appeared to Paul in the night; There stood a man of
Macedonia, and prayed him, saying, Come over into Macedonia,
and help us. [10] And after he had seen the vision, immediately we
endeavoured to go into Macedonia, assuredly gathering that the Lord
had called us for to preach the gospel unto them.

1 CORINTHIANS 16:9

For a great door and effectual is opened unto me, and there are
many adversaries.

LOOK FOR SOMETHING MORE

LESSON 6.1

The Lord commanded the disciples to cross over to the other side. Therefore, they were there at God's bidding. They had started to obey Him, which is the reason they were in the storm.

Not all the storms we encounter are caused by our own ignorance, unbelief, or sin. We can be perfectly led by God and still experience hardship. Satan will come against us. There will be circumstances that make it seem as though we're going to drown, but that isn't always an indication that we've missed God.

The disciples were exactly where the Lord had told them to be. He was aware of their situation. Jesus came walking on the water to them, but He would have passed them by. The Lord revealed Himself to them, but it was their responsibility to call out to Him and draw on His power by faith.

It is our responsibility too. God is with us in the midst of our situations, but we must call upon Him in faith—not desperation, bitterness, frustration, or pity. He's there to help, but we have to call out in faith.

We also need to recognize that the Lord walked on top of the situation that could have destroyed the disciples. God is not overwhelmed by our problems. He's cool. He's on top of it. Nothing is impossible for God!

> *Be of good cheer: it is I; be not afraid.*
>
> Mark 6:50

Jesus told the disciples to be of good cheer, or rejoice, before the wind ceased, while the adverse situation was still going on around them. You must operate in faith before you see your deliverance—not afterward! Most people today call out for help in desperation, pity, anger, and frustration, but not really in faith. How can you tell if you're in faith—true faith? You'll be abounding in thanksgiving, full of good cheer, and not afraid (Col. 2:7 and Mark 6:50).

Now, if you're struggling with your emotions or fighting off some fears, it doesn't mean that you're totally not in faith. Don't think that! What I'm saying is that you're not yet abounding in faith. If you are still struggling with all of those things, then your faith hasn't been made perfect yet. The good news is that you can overcome that and begin rejoicing in the midst of your problem anyway. In fact, you don't always have to have perfect faith to be able to see your deliverance manifest, yet you should be shooting for abounding faith. You must learn to operate in faith before you see your deliverance—not afterward!

UNPLUG

The Lord told the disciples to be of good courage because it was Him.

> *Jesus spake unto them, saying, Be of good cheer; it is I; be not afraid.*
> *[28] And Peter answered him and said, Lord, if it be thou, bid me come*
> *unto thee on the water.*
>
> Matthew 14:27-28

Remember, the disciples were in the boat and had spent somewhere between seven and twelve hours trying to get across the Sea of Galilee. Normally, the entire trip would have taken only about two or three hours, but there they were, only halfway across the lake. In the midst of everything, Jesus came to them, walking on the water. They saw Him and cried out in fear. He basically said, "Guys, be of good cheer. It's Me. Don't be afraid!" Essentially, Peter responded, "If it's You, Lord, bid me to come to You on the water."

OUTLINE

I.   The Lord commanded the disciples to cross over to the other side; therefore, they were there at God's bidding.

   A. Not all the storms we encounter are caused by our own ignorance, unbelief, or sin.

      i.   We can be perfectly led by God and still experience hardship.

      ii. Satan will come against us.

   B. There will be circumstances that make it seem as though we're going to drown, but that isn't always an indication that we've missed God.

      i.   The disciples were exactly where the Lord had told them to be—He was aware of their situation.

   C. Jesus came walking on the water to them, but would have passed them by.

   D. The Lord revealed Himself to them, but it was their responsibility to call out to Him and draw on His power by faith.

   E. God is with us in the midst of our situations, but we must call upon Him in faith—not desperation, bitterness, frustration, or pity.

   F. He's there to help, but we have to call out in faith.

II. We also need to recognize that the Lord walked on top of the situation that could have destroyed the disciples.

   A. God is not overwhelmed by our problems.

      Be of good cheer: it is I; be not afraid.

                                                                    Mark 6:50

   B. Jesus told them this while the adverse situation was still going on around them.

      i.   We must operate in faith before we see our deliverance—not afterward!

   C. Most people today call out for help in desperation, pity, anger, and frustration, but not really in faith.

D. If we're in true faith, we'll be abounding in thanksgiving, full of good cheer, and not afraid (Col. 2:7 and Mark 6:50).

III. If you're struggling with your emotions or fighting off some fears, it doesn't mean that you're totally not in faith.

  A. If you are still struggling with all of those things, then your faith hasn't been made perfect yet.

  B. The good news is that you can overcome that and begin rejoicing in the midst of your problem anyway.

  C. You don't always have to have perfect faith to be able to see your deliverance manifest, yet you should be shooting for abounding faith.

IV. The disciples were in the boat and had spent somewhere between seven and twelve hours trying to get across the Sea of Galilee (Matt. 14:27-28).

  A. Normally, the entire trip would have taken only about two or three hours, but there they were, only halfway across the lake.

  B. In the midst of everything, Jesus came to them, walking on the water.

  C. They saw Him and cried out in fear.

  D. He basically said, "Guys, be of good cheer. It's Me. Don't be afraid!"

  E. Essentially, Peter responded, "If it's You, Lord, bid me to come to You on the water."

TEACHER'S GUIDE

1. The Lord commanded the disciples to cross over to the other side; therefore, they were there at God's bidding. Not all the storms we encounter are caused by our own ignorance, unbelief, or sin. We can be perfectly led by God and still experience hardship. Satan will come against us. There will be circumstances that make it seem as though we're going to drown, but that isn't always an indication that we've missed God. The disciples were exactly where the Lord had told them to be—He was aware of their situation. Jesus came walking on the water to them, but would have passed them by. The Lord revealed Himself to them, but it was their responsibility to call out to Him and draw on His power by faith. God is with us in the midst of our situations, but we must call upon Him in faith—not desperation, bitterness, frustration, or pity. He's there to help, but we have to call out in faith.

1a. True or false: The disciples were following the Lord's direction by crossing to the other side by boat.
   True
1b. You can be perfectly led by God and still experience _____.
   Hardship
1c. Where is God in the midst of your situation?
   God is with you

2. We also need to recognize that the Lord walked on top of the situation that could have destroyed the disciples. God is not overwhelmed by our problems.

> *Be of good cheer: it is I; be not afraid.*
>
>   Mark 6:50

Jesus told them this while the adverse situation was still going on around them. We must operate in faith before we see our deliverance—not afterward! Most people today call out for help in desperation, pity, anger, and frustration, but not really in faith. If we're in true faith, we'll be abounding in thanksgiving, full of good cheer, and not afraid (Col. 2:7 and Mark 6:50).

2a. Why was the Lord able to walk on top of a situation that could have destroyed the disciples?
   God is not overwhelmed by your problems
2b. What did Jesus say (in contemporary language) to the disciples when He got close to them?

    A. "I'm on My way"
    B. "It's Me; don't be afraid"
    C. "Be glad"
    D. A and B
    E. B and C
    E. B and C

2c. True or false: Jesus told the disciples to rejoice and be glad while the storm was still going on around them.
    True

2d. You must operate in faith _____ you see your deliverance.
    Before

2e. In a storm, you know you are in true faith when—
    A. You're abounding in thanksgiving
    B. You're full of good cheer
    C. You're not afraid
    D. All of the above
    E. None of the above
    D. All of the above

3. If we're struggling with our emotions or fighting off some fears, it doesn't mean that we're totally not in faith. If we're still struggling with all of those things, then our faith hasn't been made perfect yet. The good news is that we can overcome that and begin rejoicing in the midst of our problem anyway. We don't always have to have perfect faith to be able to see our deliverance manifest, yet we should be shooting for abounding faith.

3a. True or false: If you are struggling with your emotions, you are not in faith.
    False

3b. *Discussion question:* Describe a time when you have seen abounding faith affect the outcome of a situation.
    Discussion question

3c. *Discussion question:* Who in the Bible had faith under pressure, and how has their example helped you grow?
    Discussion question

4. The disciples were in the boat and had spent somewhere between seven and twelve hours trying to get across the Sea of Galilee (Matt. 14:27-28). Normally, the entire trip would have taken only about two or three hours, but there they were, only halfway across the lake. In the midst of everything, Jesus came to them, walking on the water. They saw Him and cried out in fear. Jesus basically said, "Guys, be of good cheer. It's Me. Don't be afraid!" Essentially, Peter responded, "If it's You, Lord, bid me to come to You on the water."

4a. Under normal circumstances, how long would a trip across the Sea of Galilee have taken?

Two or three hours

4b. How do you know the disciples were struggling on the sea of Galilee?
   A. They had spent somewhere between seven and twelve hours trying to get across
   B. They had put on their life jackets
   C. They were all paddling
   D. All of the above
   E. None of the above

   A. They had spent somewhere between seven and twelve hours trying to get across

4c. *Discussion question:* Why do you think Peter had the courage to ask the Lord to tell him to come to Him on the water?

   Discussion question

DISCIPLESHIP QUESTIONS

1. True or false: The disciples were following the Lord's direction by crossing to the other side by boat.

2. You can be perfectly led by God and still experience _____.

3. Where is God in the midst of your situation?

   _____

   _____

   _____

4. Why was the Lord able to walk on top of a situation that could have destroyed the disciples?

   _____

   _____

   _____

5. What did Jesus say (in contemporary language) to the disciples when He got close to them?
   A. "I'm on My way"
   B. "It's Me; don't be afraid"
   C. "Be glad"
   D. A and B
   E. B and C

6. True or false: Jesus told the disciples to rejoice and be glad while the storm was still going on around them.

7. You must operate in faith _____ you see your deliverance.

8. In a storm, you know that you are in true faith when—
   A. You're abounding in thanksgiving
   B. You're full of good cheer
   C. You're not afraid
   D. All of the above
   E. None of the above

9.   True or false: If you are struggling with your emotions, you are not in faith.

10.   *Discussion question:* Describe a time when you have seen abounding faith affect the outcome of a situation.

   _____

   _____

   _____

11.   *Discussion question:* Who in the Bible had faith under pressure, and how has their example helped you grow?

   _____

   _____

   _____

12.   Under normal circumstances, how long would a trip across the Sea of Galilee have taken?

   _____

   _____

   _____

13.   How do you know the disciples were struggling on the Sea of Galilee?
      A.   They had spent somewhere between seven and twelve hours trying to get across
      B.   They had put on their life jackets
      C.   They were all paddling
      D.   All of the above
      E.   None of the above

14.   *Discussion question:* Why do you think Peter had the courage to ask the Lord to tell him to come to Him on the water?

   _____

   _____

   _____

ANSWER KEY

1. True

2. Hardship

3. God is with you

4. God is not overwhelmed by your problems

5. E. B and C

6. True

7. Before

8. D. All of the above

9. False

10. *Discussion question*

11. *Discussion question*

12. Two or three hours

13. A. They had spent somewhere between seven and twelve hours trying to get across

14. *Discussion question*

SCRIPTURES

MARK 6:50

For they all saw him, and were troubled. And immediately he talked with them, and saith unto them, Be of good cheer: it is I; be not afraid.

COLOSSIANS 2:7

Rooted and built up in him, and stablished in the faith, as ye have been taught, abounding therein with thanksgiving.

MATTHEW 14:27-28

But straightway Jesus spake unto them, saying, Be of good cheer; it is I; be not afraid. [28] And Peter answered him and said, Lord, if it be thou, bid me come unto thee on the water.

Look for Something More

LESSON 6.2

Peter was affected in a supernatural way by his encounter with the Lord. He was able to unplug from his own personal dilemma out in the boat and focus on the miraculous power and ability of God.

In order to become a water walker, you must first get out of your self. You must unplug from your own personal problems and the fear about what's happening to you and focus on God. You can't become so engrossed in your own problems and overwhelmed with the impossibilities you are facing that you lose sight of the Lord and what He can do.

SUCCESS EXPOSES UNBELIEF

I used to attend a ministers' breakfast every Tuesday morning when I was in town. Fifteen or twenty ministers would take turns standing up and crying about "the good old days." They'd say, "I remember when this and that used to happen here in Colorado Springs, but now it's just a preachers' graveyard. Nothing significant can happen here anymore. If you come to Colorado Springs to build a large church or ministry, you'll leave feet first. No Spirit-filled church can ever grow beyond 100 members here." They gave instances of those who had tried. Once they attained 100 or 110 people, the church would split or something else would happen. I listened to them whine about their storms—their problems—for a while without saying anything. Finally, they looked at me and asked, "Well, what do you think?"

I replied, "Guys, in the past week, I've seen blind eyes and deaf ears opened. I've personally seen miracle upon miracle. Churches all over are growing. You guys are totally wrong. You're looking at your situation and thinking that the whole body of Christ is like that. You're just looking at yourself! I don't know all the reasons you are struggling, but I can guarantee you that this isn't going on throughout the entire body of Christ. I praise God that I get to travel instead of being stuck here, hanging around your constant negativity!"

You can get to the point where you look at and think about your own situation so much that you forget the miraculous power of God. For instance, there was a young man in that ministers' group who had come to town to start a church. He was talking like he was going to have a megachurch in Colorado Springs, but the other ministers just discounted him and laughed at him. Yet he and I became instant friends because we were both believing God for something big and looking for something more.

When that fellow first came to town, he stepped right into the middle of a very negative situation. While others focused on what had happened in the past and weren't able to see outside the box, he was able to get outside of his limitations and see beyond his own situation. He looked to God and believed Him. Today that young man pastors a church that serves thousands of people.

DESTROYED OR MOTIVATED?

Peter was just as caught up in the situation as everyone else on the boat. However, when Jesus appeared, he started believing God for something greater. He began thinking, *If Jesus can walk on water, so can I*. He responded positively when the Lord told him to be of good cheer and not to be afraid. Peter believed Christ's words and began to act upon them.

As a result, Peter was able to rise above his present situation. The boisterous wind and surging waves weren't the main issue. Peter realized that God was with him and that His power was available to him. So, he began to respond to that and look for something more. If you're going to be a water walker, you must get your focus off your circumstances and look to God for something more!

Negative circumstances in your life have the potential to either destroy you or motivate you. For example, I once dated a girl who was later diagnosed with leukemia. We all believed it was God's will to heal her, yet she died. Although that negative situation nearly overwhelmed me, stunted my spiritual growth, and stopped me from doing anything for the Lord, I decided to seek Him even more instead. I purposed in my heart that I would see the miraculous power of God.

Like Peter, I looked to Jesus and responded positively to His words, instead of looking at the negative circumstances. We may have lost that battle, but I knew that someday I would see the same thing that killed that girl—leukemia—beaten, and I have, many times over! But first, I had to get the attitude that there was more of God available than what I was presently experiencing. Like Peter, I had to choose a different attitude than the rest of the guys in the boat. When Peter did that, he stepped out and walked on the water!

"THERE MUST BE MORE!"

While growing up, John G. Lake saw eight of his siblings—four brothers and four sisters—die prematurely due to sickness. For thirty-two years, there was always at least one member of his family who was an invalid. When his young wife took ill and was on the verge of death, Lake cried out to God, asking, "Why are You letting this happen?"

The Lord answered, saying, "It's not Me who is letting this happen. You are! This isn't My will. Satan is killing the members of your family prematurely, and it's your responsibility to do something about it. You have the authority to heal these people!"

John G. Lake heard God, believed, and saw his wife raised up. He began a miracle ministry that saw well over 100,000 documented cases of divine healing. At one time, Spokane, Washington, was declared the healthiest city in the United States, and they credited this to his ministry.

All the sickness, death, and loss could have just overwhelmed and sunk Lake, but he became motivated to seek God and His Word. He declared, "There must be more! I will see the miraculous power of God manifest in my life!" And he did.

"TRUST ME"

That's what Peter did; he trusted God. Jesus appeared and spoke, "Be of good cheer. It's Me. Don't be afraid!" In essence, the Lord was saying, "Trust Me; power is available." Peter responded positively and started believing for something more. He was able to look past the howling wind and cresting waves. He looked past the things in the natural realm and focused his attention on Jesus.

Are you able to look past the circumstances in your life? Can you get out of your boat of self-pity and look to the Lord? Are you able to look past your situation and see that God is victorious and well able to give you hope and encouragement? Or are you going to sit there and let the circumstances of life overcome you?

These are questions that must be answered if you are going to walk on water and see miracles in your life. You must first of all lift your head up and start looking for something else. You have to have hope that there is something more than what you're experiencing. Shake yourself! Get out of the frustration, discouragement, and despair. Decide to overcome. God's power is truly what delivers you, but it's activated by what you choose to believe. Peter wasn't ready to believe God fully at that exact moment, but he at least called out to Jesus and started making a demand on God's power. Will you do the same?

OUTLINE

V. Peter was affected in a supernatural way by his encounter with the Lord.

    A. He was able to unplug from his own personal dilemma out in the boat and focus on the miraculous power and ability of God.

    B. In order to become a water walker, you must first get out of your self.

    C. You must unplug from your own personal problems and the fear about what's happening to you and focus on God.

    D. You can't become so engrossed in your own problems that you lose sight of the Lord and what He can do.

VI. Peter was just as caught up in the situation as everyone else on the boat.

    A. However, when Jesus appeared, he started believing God for something greater.

    B. He responded positively when the Lord told him to be of good cheer and not to be afraid.

    C. Peter realized that God was with him and that His power was available to him.

    D. So, he began to respond to that and look for something more.

    E. If you're going to be a water walker, you must get your focus off your circumstances and look to God for something more!

VII. Negative circumstances in your life have the potential to either destroy you or motivate you.

    A. For example, I once dated a girl who was later diagnosed with leukemia.

    B. We believed it was God's will to heal her, yet she died.

        i. Although that negative situation nearly overwhelmed me, stunted my spiritual growth, and stopped me from doing anything for the Lord, I purposed in my heart that I would see the miraculous power of God.

      ii. Like Peter, I looked to Jesus and responded positively to His words, instead of looking at the negative circumstances.

  C. We may have lost that battle, but I knew that someday I would see the same thing that killed that girl—leukemia—beaten, and I have, many times over!

  D. But first, I had to get the attitude that there was more of God available than what I was presently experiencing.

  E. Peter had to choose a different attitude than the rest of the guys in the boat; when he did, he stepped out and walked on the water!

VIII. Peter trusted God.

  A. He looked past the things in the natural realm and focused his attention on Jesus.

  B. Are you able to look past the circumstances in your life?

      i. Can you get out of your boat of self-pity and look to the Lord?

      ii. Are you able to look past your situation and see that God is victorious and well able to give you hope and encouragement?

  C. Or are you going to sit there and let the circumstances of life overcome you?

IX. If you are going to walk on water and see miracles in your life, you must first of all lift your head up and start looking for something else.

  A. You have to have hope that there is something more than what you're experiencing.

  B. Get out of the frustration, discouragement, and despair—decide to overcome.

  C. God's power is truly what delivers you, but it's activated by what you choose to believe.

  D. Peter wasn't ready to believe God fully at that exact moment, but he at least called out to Jesus and started making a demand on God's power.

  E. Will you do the same?

TEACHER'S GUIDE

5. Peter was affected in a supernatural way by his encounter with the Lord. He was able to unplug from his own personal dilemma out in the boat and focus on the miraculous power and ability of God. In order to become water walkers, we must first get out of our selves. We must unplug from our own personal problems and the fear about what's happening to us and focus on God. We can't become so engrossed in our own problems that we lose sight of the Lord and what He can do.

5a. True or false: Peter was affected supernaturally when he encountered the Lord during the storm.
    True

5b. What was Peter able to focus on that allowed him to become a water walker?
    A. Himself
    B. The miraculous power and ability of God
    C. The storm
    D. All of the above
    E. None of the above
    B. The miraculous power and ability of God

5c. *Discussion question:* What happens when you become engrossed in your own problems in the storm?
    Discussion question

6. Peter was just as caught up in the situation as everyone else on the boat. However, when Jesus appeared, he started believing God for something greater. He responded positively when the Lord told him to be of good cheer and not to be afraid. Peter realized that God was with him and that His power was available to him. So, he began to respond to that and look for something more. If we're going to be water walkers, we must get our focus off our circumstances and look to God for something more!

6a. True or false: Peter wasn't caught up in the storm; he wasn't like everyone else in the boat.
    False

6b. Peter started to believe God for something greater when _____ appeared.
    Jesus

6c. *Discussion question:* What does Peter's response teach us about Jesus' presence in the storms of our lives?
    Discussion question

6d. What do you have to do if you're going to become a water walker?
    Get your focus off your circumstances and look to God

7. Negative circumstances in our lives have the potential to either destroy us or motivate us. For example, Andrew once dated a girl who was later diagnosed with leukemia. They believed it was God's will to heal her, yet she died. Although that negative situation nearly overwhelmed Andrew, stunted his spiritual growth, and stopped him from doing anything for the Lord, he purposed in his heart that he would see the miraculous power of God. Like Peter, he looked to Jesus and responded positively to His words, instead of looking at the negative circumstances. They might have lost that battle, but Andrew knew that someday he would see the same thing that killed that girl—leukemia—beaten, and he has, many times over! But first, he had to get the attitude that there was more of God available than what he was presently experiencing. Peter had to choose a different attitude than the rest of the guys in the boat; when he did, he stepped out and walked on the water!

7a. True or false: Negative circumstances can either destroy you or motivate you.
    True
7b. How was Andrew's response like Peter's in this situation?
    He responded positively to the Word, instead of looking at the
    negative circumstances

8. Peter trusted God. He looked past the things in the natural realm and focused his attention on Jesus. Are we able to look past the circumstances in our lives? Can we get out of our boats of self-pity and look to the Lord? Are we able to look past our situations and see that God is victorious and well able to give us hope and encouragement? Or are we going to sit there and let the circumstances of life overcome us?

8a. Peter trusted God—how did he show that?
    A. He started a 501(c)3
    B. He looked at the natural realm and changed his mind about walking to Jesus
    C. He looked past the natural realm and focused his attention on Jesus
    D. All of the above
    E. None of the above
    C. He looked past the natural realm and focused his attention on Jesus
8b. *Discussion question:* What are some ways you can get out of your boat of self-pity and look to the Lord?
    Discussion question

9. If we are going to walk on water and see miracles in our lives, we must first of all lift our heads up and start looking for something else. We have to have hope that there is something more than what we're experiencing. Let's get out of the frustration, discouragement, and despair—we should decide to overcome. God's power is truly what delivers us, but it's activated by what we choose to believe. Peter wasn't ready to

believe God fully at that exact moment, but he at least called out to Jesus and started making a demand on God's power. Will we do the same?

9a. According to the lesson, what do you have to have hope for?
  A. That there is something more than what you're expecting
  B. That your lottery numbers will come up
  C. That your boat won't sink
  D. All of the above
  E. None of the above
  A. That there is something more than what you're expecting
9b. God's power is truly what _____ you.
  Delivers
9c. How is God's power activated?
  By what you choose to believe

DISCIPLESHIP QUESTIONS

15. True or false: Peter was affected supernaturally when he encountered the Lord during the storm.

16. What was Peter able to focus on that allowed him to become a water walker?
    A.   Himself
    B.   The miraculous power and ability of God
    C.   The storm
    D.   All of the above
    E.   None of the above

17. *Discussion question:* What happens when you become engrossed in your own problems in the storm?

    _____

    _____

    _____

18. True or false: Peter wasn't caught up in the storm; he wasn't like everyone else in the boat.

19. Peter started to believe God for something greater when _____ appeared.

20. *Discussion question:* What does Peter's response teach us about Jesus' presence in the storms of our lives?

    _____

    _____

    _____

21. What do you have to do if you're going to become a water walker?

    _____

    _____

    _____

22. True or false: Negative circumstances can either destroy you or motivate you.

23. How was Andrew's response like Peter's in this situation?

_____

_____

_____

24. Peter trusted God—how did he show that?
    A.   He started a 501(c)3
    B.   He looked at the natural realm and changed his mind about walking to Jesus
    C.   He looked past the natural realm and focused his attention on Jesus
    D.   All of the above
    E.   None of the above

25. *Discussion question:* What are some ways you can get out of your boat of self-pity and look to the Lord?

_____

_____

_____

26. According to the lesson, what do you have to have hope for?
    A.   That there is something more than what you're expecting
    B.   That your lottery numbers will come up
    C.   That your boat won't sink
    D.   All of the above
    E.   None of the above

27. God's power is truly what _____ you.

28. How is God's power activated?

_____

_____

_____

Answer Key

15. True

16. B. The miraculous power and ability of God

17. *Discussion question*

18. False

19. Jesus

20. *Discussion question*

21. Get your focus off your circumstances and look to God

22. True

23. He responded positively to the Word, instead of looking at the negative circumstances

24. C. He looked past the natural realm and focused his attention on Jesus

25. *Discussion question*

26. A. That there is something more than what you're expecting

27. Delivers

28. By what you choose to believe

How Are You Asking?

LESSON 7

And Peter answered him and said, Lord, if it be thou, bid me come unto thee on the water.

Matthew 14:28

Although his intent was good, notice how Peter worded this question. Basically, he was saying, "Lord, if You can walk on the water, I can too. I want to do that!" Peter desired to do what Jesus was doing and walk in the miraculous. That was good, but the way he asked this question was incorrect.

There is no other recorded instance in Scripture—or history—of anyone walking on water. This is it, right here, with Jesus and Peter! Moses, Elijah, and Elisha all parted water and walked across on dry ground, but nobody else ever walked on water. Perhaps it wasn't really God's plan for Peter to walk on water. It was certainly possible, because the Lord wouldn't have allowed him to come otherwise, but this wasn't necessarily God's best.

If Peter had asked the question differently and said "Lord, do You want me to walk on the water with You?" it's possible he would have received a different answer. Jesus could have responded, "Well, Peter, I'll come to you. Then we'll go to the other side and everything will be just fine."

It's possible that Peter's faith wasn't totally up to walking on the water and enduring all the unbelief that would come from that action. But Peter specifically asked, "Lord, if it's You, bid me come to You on the water." What else could the Lord say? "Don't come. It's not Me!"? No, it was Him! The way Peter asked the question left Jesus no option for a different answer.

"SHOULD I STAY?"

It's important how you ask God questions and discern His will for your life. Years ago, when I was still in the Baptist church, I began getting a hold of faith teaching and started sharing it. Of course, I received a lot of criticism for that. Due to the constant conflict, there were many times during those two years that I thought about leaving the Baptist church and just going on with God.

That was around 1970, when there weren't yet any independent, Spirit-filled churches around. Pentecostal-type churches certainly believed in the baptism in the Holy Spirit and praying in tongues, but they were anti-charismatic. In fact, they were some of the biggest persecutors of the charismatic church. Therefore, there was nothing except the established denominational churches. Independent, Spirit-filled churches didn't exist back then, and it was a major step to leave your denominational church.

The constant barrage of criticism hindered and hurt me, but I stayed at my denominational church for over two years because of the way I asked God my question: "Lord, do You want me to just leave the Baptist church and let them go to hell? Don't You care? Don't You want me to stay here and minister to these people?"

How else could God answer that question? "Yes, Andrew. Leave the Baptist church and let all the people there go to hell because I don't care about them." Certainly not! God loves Baptists. He loves everyone attending a denominational church. But because of the way I asked my question, the Lord couldn't tell me to leave.

Looking back on things, I personally believe God was leading me to move on. He wanted me to follow Him into the baptism in the Holy Spirit, speaking in tongues, the gifts of the Holy Spirit, and miracles. I praise God for all of the good that came into my life through my denominational heritage—and I love the Baptists—but I personally could not go on with the Lord in that particular church environment.

Finally, it got to the point one day when I just asked, "God, do You want me to stay in this church or not?"

Immediately, He answered, "No. Leave." And I left. That was the beginning of a major shift for good in my life. I realized that I had hindered myself from taking this step earlier because of how I had asked my question. You need to be careful how you ask your question!

NONE OF THE ABOVE!

Many years ago, a young man from Oklahoma Baptist University (OBU) became excited after visiting the church I was pastoring in Seagoville, Texas. He told me that although he very much wanted to come sit under the Word and let me disciple him, he had a problem. He had prayed and asked God to specifically guide him about where he was supposed to go to school. He received a scholarship to OBU. He'd only been there about six to eight weeks when he decided that he wanted to leave all of that behind and come sit under my ministry. But he was confused and said, "God, I know You led me to OBU and provided a scholarship for me, but now I feel like You're leading me down to Seagoville, Texas. How could You do that?"

He struggled with that for about three months before he came to me and said, "The Lord has answered my question. He told me, 'Out of the two choices you gave Me—Berkeley or Oklahoma Baptist University—OBU was better. But if you could have heard Me, I would have told you that I wanted you to go sit under Andrew's ministry instead.'" Basically, God was telling him, "Instead of only saying, (A) Berkeley or (B) OBU, you should have included (C) None of the above!"

This is why we sometimes miss out on hearing God's voice. We say, "God, do You want me to do (A) or (B)?" But you ought to also give Him the option of "(C) None of the above." Just ask Him, "Lord, is there anything I'm missing?"

"COME!"

Peter didn't do that. He just said, "Lord, if it's You, bid me to come!" It really doesn't do us any good to speculate about what could have or should have happened. We don't know what God's original plan or intent might have been. Was Peter really mature enough to handle the situation or not? All we can do is guess. But the way he asked the question left Jesus no room to say anything except *Come* (Matt. 14:29). If we are believing God for something miraculous and are about to take the biggest step of our lives, we need to make sure that it's God leading us to do it, instead of us backing God into a corner and leaving Him no other option.

One of my friends is a wonderful guy who has always been totally in love with the Lord and committed to Him. However, earlier in his life he thought that the only way he could really serve God was as a full-time minister. So, he went on staff with a church and poured himself into running a Christian school for a number of years. Although he did excellent work, he still went back into the secular world to work a regular job. When I saw him recently, he told me, "Andrew, I was mistaken. I thought the only way I could serve God was as a full-time minister. However, I'm happier and more fulfilled now than I've ever been. In fact, I'm actually reaching out and leading people to the Lord from work. God is so good!"

Are you asking God something like, "Do You want me to serve You by being in full-time ministry, or not serve You at all?" Well, if that's the way you phrase your question, God's going to say, "Serve Me." But it's possible He would prefer that you stay in the business world and serve Him that way. You need to be careful that you are truly being led by God in what you want to step out of the boat and believe for and that you're not just misunderstanding, confusing, and phrasing things in an incorrect way.

OUTLINE

I.   Although his intent was good, notice how Peter worded this question:

And Peter answered him and said, Lord, if it be thou, bid me come unto thee on the water.

Matthew 14:28

A. Peter desired to walk in the miraculous, but the way he asked this question was incorrect.

B. Perhaps it wasn't really God's plan for Peter to walk on water—this wasn't necessarily God's best.

C. It's possible that Peter's faith wasn't totally up to walking on the water and enduring all the unbelief that would come from that action, but Peter specifically asked, "Lord, if it's You, bid me come to You on the water."

D. The way Peter asked the question left Jesus no option for a different answer.

II. It's important how you ask God questions and discern His will for your life.

A. You need to be careful how you ask your question.

B. If you are believing God for something miraculous, you need to make sure it's God leading you to do it, instead of you backing Him into a corner.

C. Are you asking God something like, "Do You want me to serve You by being in full-time ministry, or not serve You at all?"

D. If that's the way you phrase your question, He's going to say, "Serve Me."

E. You need to be careful that you are truly being led by God in what you want to step out of the boat and believe for, and that you're not just misunderstanding, confusing, and phrasing things in an incorrect way.

TEACHER'S GUIDE

1. Although his intent was good, notice how Peter worded this question:

    And Peter answered him and said, Lord, if it be thou, bid me come unto thee on the water.

    Matthew 14:28

Peter desired to walk in the miraculous, but the way he asked this question was incorrect. Perhaps it wasn't really God's plan for Peter to walk on water—this wasn't necessarily God's best. It's possible that Peter's faith wasn't totally up to walking on the water and enduring all the unbelief that would come from that action, but Peter specifically asked, "Lord, if it's You, bid me come to You on the water." The way Peter asked the question left Jesus no option for a different answer.

1a. True or false: Perhaps it wasn't really God's plan for Peter to walk on water.
   True

1b. Peter specifically asked, "Lord, if _____, bid me come to You on the water."
   A. "it's You"
   B. "it's Your will"
   C. "I am worthy"
   D. "I have the faith"
   E. "You are divine"
   A. "it's You"

1c. *Discussion question:* How did Peter ask the wrong question?
   Discussion question

1d. *Discussion question:* How can you ask God good questions?
   Discussion question

2. It's important how we ask God questions and discern His will for our lives. We need to be careful how we ask our question. If we are believing God for something miraculous, we need to make sure it's God leading us to do it, instead of us backing Him into a corner. Are we asking God something like, "Do You want us to serve You by being in full-time ministry, or not serve You at all?" If that's the way we phrase our question, He's going to say, "Serve Me." We need to be careful that we are truly being led by God in what we want to step out of the boat and believe for, and that we're not just misunderstanding, confusing, and phrasing things in an incorrect way.

2a. Why should you be careful how you ask God questions?
   You can back Him into a corner

2b. Why do you need to be careful that you are truly being led by God in what you want to step out of the boat and believe for?

<u>You could be misunderstanding, confusing, and phrasing things in an incorrect way</u>

2c. *Discussion question:* How do you discern God's will for your life?

<u>Discussion question</u>

2d. *Discussion question:* What are you believing God for?

<u>Discussion question</u>

DISCIPLESHIP QUESTIONS

1. True or false: Perhaps it wasn't really God's plan for Peter to walk on water.

2. Peter specifically asked, "Lord, if _____, bid me come to You on the water."
    A. "it's You"
    B. "it's Your will"
    C. "I am worthy"
    D. "I have the faith"
    E. "You are divine"

3. *Discussion question:* How did Peter ask the wrong question?

    _____

    _____

    _____

4. *Discussion question:* How can you ask God good questions?

    _____

    _____

    _____

5. Why should you be careful how you ask God questions?

    _____

    _____

    _____

6. Why do you need to be careful that you are truly being led by God in what you want to step out of the boat and believe for?

    _____

    _____

    _____

7.   *Discussion question:* How do you discern God's will for your life?

_____

_____

_____

8.   *Discussion question:* What are you believing God for?

_____

_____

_____

ANSWER KEY

1. True

2. A. "it's You"

3. *Discussion question*

4. *Discussion question*

5. You can back Him into a corner

6. You could be misunderstanding, confusing, and phrasing things in an incorrect way

7. *Discussion question*

8. *Discussion question*

SCRIPTURES

MATTHEW 14:28-29

And Peter answered him and said, Lord, if it be thou, bid me come unto thee on the water. [29] And he said, Come. And when Peter was come down out of the ship, he walked on the water, to go to Jesus.

GET OUT OF THE BOAT

LESSON 8.1

And he said, Come. And when Peter was come down out of the ship, he walked on the water, to go to Jesus.

Matthew 14:29

Peter had taken his attention off the howling wind and swirling water—everything that was hindering them from making it to the other side—and was looking at Jesus. He was believing that he could do miraculous things. He had asked, and God had given him the command—"Come!"

One word from Jesus is enough to overcome whatever circumstance, situation, or problem is trying to destroy us. One word! And the good news is that we have lots of words in the Bible. Just one word quickened to us—made alive—is enough to overcome any storm, or problem, we may encounter in our lives. That's powerful!

Sometimes we think, *I must read volumes of Scripture in order to build my faith. I have to spend fifteen hours a day studying God's Word,* when, in fact, just one scripture—one word from God—can quicken our faith. It's not always the quantity that makes the difference; rather, it's how much that one thing that God has spoken means to us.

I've sat beside people in services who have heard the exact same message I did. They may have been a little blessed, but they just went on about their life without realizing how powerful the word they heard really was. Yet I sat there and meditated on it until that word exploded on the inside of me. That person had the same ability to receive from that word as I did, but it just didn't impact them the same.

POWER IN THE WORD

You might think that the word *"come"* isn't a very important word. But it was spoken by the Creator—the One who created everything natural, including the water and the wind. That one word had enough power in it for Peter to walk on water.

Likewise, the promises God has given you have enough power for you to accomplish whatever He's told you to do.

If God has called you to be a minister, then *"faithful is he that calleth you, who also will do it"* (1 Thess. 5:24). Paul said,

> *I thank Christ Jesus our Lord, who hath enabled me, for that he counted me faithful, putting me into the ministry.*
>
> 1 Timothy 1:12

You'll discover that when God calls you, He's already seen you as faithful, or He wouldn't have called you. In other words, the Lord has faith in you. If God has faith in you, then you ought to have faith in yourself. If you would meditate on this, you'd realize that when God called you, there was more to that call than what you may have recognized. If God has faith in you, then you need to put some faith in you and in the ability of God on the inside of you. You can do whatever the Lord has called you to do!

If God has called you to healing and you haven't seen it yet, then look at the scripture that says, *"By [His] stripes ye were healed"* (1 Pet. 2:24, brackets mine). There is more than enough power to overcome whatever problem you may have—sickness, financial, relationship, etc. The Word of God has more than enough power, but you must step out and act on it in faith.

There were twelve guys in that boat, but only one of them walked on water. Every one of them could have done that. Now, again, I'm not sure that was God's best, but Peter called out and said "If it's You, bid me come" and the Lord let him. Every one of those disciples could have said that and done the same thing! Yet most people never get out of the boat because of fear. They simply refuse to take that step of faith.

People say things like, "Well, it's normal for us to get sick every fall and winter. You have to expect things like the flu. As you get older, your health starts deteriorating. You just have to allow for those kinds of things." That's how the world thinks; that's the world's boat!

We sing songs that say, "Lord, I'm only human. I'm just a man." That's not a very good song for a Christian to sing, because we are not only human—one-third of us is wall-to-wall Holy Ghost! We need to start believing for something more. We need to get out of the boat!

OUTLINE

I. Peter had taken his attention off everything that was hindering them from making it to the other side and was looking at Jesus.

> *And he said, Come. And when Peter was come down out of the ship, he walked on the water, to go to Jesus.*
>
> Matthew 14:29

A. Peter was believing that he could do miraculous things.

B. One word from Jesus is enough to overcome whatever circumstance, situation, or problem is trying to destroy us.

C. Sometimes we think, *I must read volumes of Scripture in order to build my faith. I have to spend fifteen hours a day studying God's Word,* when, in fact, just one scripture—one word from God—can quicken our faith.

D. It's not always the quantity that makes the difference; rather, it's how much that one thing that God has spoken means to us.

II. You might think that the word *"come"* isn't a very important word, but it was spoken by the Creator—the One who created everything natural, including the water and the wind.

A. That one word had enough power in it for Peter to walk on water.

B. Likewise, the promises God has given you have enough power for you to accomplish whatever He's told you to do.

C. If God has called you to be a minister, then *"faithful is he that calleth you, who also will do it"* (1 Thess. 5:24).

D. Paul said,

> *I thank Christ Jesus our Lord, who hath enabled me, for that he counted me faithful, putting me into the ministry.*
>
> 1 Timothy 1:12

E. You'll discover that when God calls you, He's already seen you as faithful, or He wouldn't have called you.

III. If God has faith in you, then you ought to have faith in yourself.

    A. If you would meditate on this, you'd realize that when God called you, there was more to that call than what you may have recognized.

    B. You need to put some faith in you and in the ability of God on the inside of you—you can do whatever the Lord has called you to do!

    C. The Word of God has more than enough power, but you must step out and act on it in faith.

IV. There were twelve guys in that boat—only one of them walked on water, but every one of them could have done that.

    A. Now, again, I'm not sure that was God's best, but Peter called out and said "If it's You, bid me come" and the Lord let him.

    B. Every one of those disciples could have said that and done the same thing!

    C. Yet most people never get out of the boat because of fear—they simply refuse to take that step of faith.

    D. We need to start believing for something more and get out of the boat!

TEACHER'S GUIDE

1. Peter had taken his attention off everything that was hindering them from making it to the other side and was looking at Jesus.

> *And he said, Come. And when Peter was come down out of the ship, he walked on the water, to go to Jesus.*
>
> Matthew 14:29

Peter was believing that he could do miraculous things. One word from Jesus is enough to overcome whatever circumstance, situation, or problem is trying to destroy us. Sometimes we think, *I must read volumes of Scripture in order to build my faith. I have to spend fifteen hours a day studying God's Word,* when, in fact, just one scripture—one word from God—can quicken our faith. It's not always the quantity that makes the difference; rather, it's how much that one thing that God has spoken means to us.

1a. Peter had taken his _____ off everything that was hindering them and was _____ at Jesus.
   Attention / looking

1b. What can quicken your faith?
   A. Reading volumes of Scripture
   B. One word from Jesus
   C. Studying God's Word for hours a day
   D. All of the above
   E. None of the above
   B. One word from Jesus

1c. True or false: How much God says to you is not what makes the difference; rather, it's how much what He says *means to you* that makes the difference.
   True

2. We might think that the word *"come"* isn't a very important word, but it was spoken by the Creator—the One who created everything natural, including the water and the wind. That one word had enough power in it for Peter to walk on water. Likewise, the promises God has given us have enough power for us to accomplish whatever He's told us to do. If God has called us to be a minister, then *"faithful is he that calleth you, who also will do it"* (1 Thess. 5:24). Paul said,

> *I thank Christ Jesus our Lord, who hath enabled me, for that he counted me faithful, putting me into the ministry.*
>
> 1 Timothy 1:12

We'll discover that when God calls us, He's already seen us as faithful, or He wouldn't have called us.

2a. True or false: The word *"come"* might not seem like a very important word—unless it is spoken to you by the Creator of the universe.
True

2b. The word *"come"* had enough _____ in it for Peter to walk on the water.
Power

2c. What do the promises of God contain that enables you to accomplish whatever He has told you to do?
Power

2d. *Discussion question:* When God calls you, He has already seen you as faithful; what does that show you about the call of God on your life?
Discussion question

3. If God has faith in us, then we ought to have faith in ourselves. If we would meditate on this, we'd realize that when God called us, there was more to that call than what we may have recognized. We need to put some faith in ourselves and in the ability of God on the inside of us—we can do whatever the Lord has called us to do! The Word of God has more than enough power, but we must step out and act on it in faith.

3a. The Word of God has more than enough power, but you must _____ _____ and act on it in faith.
Step out

4. There were twelve guys in that boat—only one of them walked on water, but every one of them could have done that. Now, again, Andrew is not sure that was God's best, but Peter called out and said "If it's You, bid me come" and the Lord let him. Every one of those disciples could have said that and done the same thing! Yet most people never get out of the boat because of fear—they simply refuse to take that step of faith. We need to start believing for something more and get out of the boat!

4a. True or false: Out of the twelve disciples who were in the boat, Peter was the only one who could have walked on the water.
False

4b. Why do most people never get out of the boat?
Fear

4c. People often simply _____ to take a step of faith to get out of the boat.
Refuse

4d. *Discussion question:* What are some ways that you can "get out of the boat" in your life?

Discussion question

DISCIPLESHIP QUESTIONS

1. Peter had taken his _____ off everything that was hindering them and was _____ at Jesus.

2. What can quicken your faith?
    A. Reading volumes of Scripture
    B. One word from Jesus
    C. Studying God's Word for hours a day
    D. All of the above
    E. None of the above

3. True or false: How much God says to you is not what makes the difference; rather it is how much what He says *means to you* that makes the difference.

4. True or false: The word *"come"* might not seem like a very important word—unless it is spoken to you by the Creator of the universe.

5. The word *"come"* had enough _____ in it for Peter to walk on the water.

6. What do the promises of God contain that enables you to accomplish whatever He has told you to do?

    _____

    _____

    _____

7. *Discussion question:* When God calls you, He has already seen you as faithful; what does that show you about the call of God on your life?

    _____

    _____

    _____

8. The Word of God has more than enough power, but you must _____ _____ and act on it in faith.

9. True or false: Out of the twelve disciples who were in the boat, Peter was the only one who could have walked on the water.

10. Why do most people never get out of the boat?

_____

_____

_____

11. People simply _____ to take a step of faith to get out of the boat.

12. *Discussion question:* What are some ways that you can "get out of the boat" in your life?

_____

_____

_____

ANSWER KEY

1. Attention / looking

2. B. One word from Jesus

3. True

4. True

5. Power

6. Power

7. *Discussion question*

8. Step out

9. False

10. Fear

11. Refuse

12. *Discussion question*

SCRIPTURES

MATTHEW 14:29

And he said, Come. And when Peter was come down out of the ship, he walked on the water, to go to Jesus.

1 THESSALONIANS 5:24

Faithful is he that calleth you, who also will do it.

1 TIMOTHY 1:12

I thank Christ Jesus our Lord, who hath enabled me, for that he counted me faithful, putting me into the ministry.

1 PETER 2:24

Who his own self bare our sins in his own body on the tree, that we, being dead to sins, should live unto righteousness: by whose stripes ye were healed.

Get Out of the Boat

LESSON 8.2

In a very real sense, people in the boat resist those who are stepping out in faith. They say, "So, are you going to just believe God? Are you really going to trust Him to supply your needs? Why not go to the banker and trust him? Are you really going to believe God instead of taking all that medicine?" Now, don't misunderstand what I'm saying. It's not a sin to do those things. It wasn't a sin for the disciples to be in the boat and start out toward the other side. But when your boat encounters a storm—when the doctor says you're going to die—why would you still keep taking their treatment if it's not working?

A friend of mine recently died of cancer. I don't understand everything involved in his situation, but I do know that he had a melanoma that just wasn't responding to treatment. He had already been through operations and chemotherapy. He'd done all this stuff, but the doctors said it wasn't helping. So, I asked him, "Why don't you just believe God?"

"No, I'm going to continue the treatments."

Again, I wasn't close enough to the situation to know exactly what happened, but when he said that, I remember thinking, *Why? They aren't doing any good!* The purpose of those treatments is to kill cells. The doctors just hope it's the cancer cells that die, but it also kills healthy cells. Those treatments take away your strength and weaken your immune system.

Some people are afraid to take a step out of the boat. They're scared of being different. They have to be like everybody else. Yet everybody else is miserable, suffering, and dying. They're just afraid to get out of the boat. Make a decision to be different. Get out of the boat! Just believe God!

"HOW LONG WILL YOU SIT THERE?"

I ministered several times to a certain man who felt like he was supposed to come to Charis Bible College. Every time we talked, he'd say "I know it's God, but..." and he would tell me about some specific fear he had. This guy had fear about his job, fear about his family, and fear about almost everything else you can imagine. Finally, I just prophesied to him using the story of the lepers at the gate of Samaria.

> *And there were four leprous men at the entering in of the gate: and they said one to another, Why sit we here until we die? [4] If we say, We will enter into the city, then the famine is in the city, and we shall die there: and if we sit still here, we die also. Now therefore come, and let us fall unto the host of the Syrians: if they save us alive, we shall live; and if they kill us, we shall but die.*

2 Kings 7:3-4

At the time, Samaria was under siege by the Syrians. These lepers—along with everyone else in the city—were dying of starvation. Finally, they basically asked, "What are we going to do? If we stay here, we're going to die. If we go into the city, we'll die because of the famine. Why don't we just get up and go out to the Syrians? If they kill us, so what? But they might feed us—and let us go!"

When the lepers went to the Syrian camp, it turned out that the Lord had caused the Syrians to hear a noise and flee. They left all their tents, gold, clothes, and food behind. Not only were these lepers fed, but they also became rich and were honored, too, because they were the ones God used to bring the good news to the rest of the city.

After I told this guy the story of the lepers, I asked, "How long are you going to sit here? Until you die? Take a step of faith in the direction you believe God wants you to go. Do something!"

RUN THE RISK

Before you can walk on the water, you have to get out of the boat. You must be willing to depart from what everybody else is doing. You have to be willing to go out and try something new. You must be willing to break with tradition, get out there, and run the risk of failure.

Many people are so afraid of failure that they continue to stay in the situation they're in, which guarantees their failure will continue. If you aren't stretching yourself and believing God for something bigger than what you can produce on your own, you're already a failure. I don't say this to condemn or hurt you but, rather, to challenge you.

God is a supernatural God! God is a big God! He is *"able to do exceeding abundantly above all that we ask or think, according to the power that worketh in us"* (Eph. 3:20).

ARE YOU NORMAL?

Is your life "normal" according to the world's system? Can anyone tell the difference between you and your neighbor? Do you go to the doctor as often as they do? Do you have the same number of bills and indebtedness as they do? Do you have the same worries and cares as they do? Are you as bothered as your unsaved friend when everything negative happens in this world? If so, something is seriously wrong.

You need to believe God for something bigger! There ought to be enough evidence to convict you if you were arrested for being a Christian. There should be something different about you compared to your unsaved neighbor. They're dead and you're alive!

Before you can see that kind of power manifest in your life, however, you need to make a conscious decision to leave the safety of the boat and get out on the water. Before you can be a water walker, you must be willing to step out of the boat. Before you can see the miraculous power of God in your life, you must be willing to run the risk!

OUTLINE

V. People in the boat resist those who are stepping out in faith.

    A. It wasn't a sin for the disciples to be in the boat and start out toward the other side.

    B. But when your boat encounters a storm—when the doctor says you're going to die—why would you still keep taking their treatment if it's not working?

    C. Some people are scared of being different—they have to be like everybody else, yet everybody else is miserable, suffering, and dying.

    D. Make a decision to be different.

    E. Just believe God!

VI. In 2 Kings 7:3-4, Samaria was under siege by the Syrians:

And there were four leprous men at the entering in of the gate: and they said one to another, Why sit we here until we die? [4] If we say, We will enter into the city, then the famine is in the city, and we shall die there: and if we sit still here, we die also. Now therefore come, and let us fall unto the host of the Syrians: if they save us alive, we shall live; and if they kill us, we shall but die.

    A. These lepers—along with everyone else in the city—were dying of starvation.

    B. When the lepers went to the Syrian camp, it turned out that the Lord had caused the Syrians to hear a noise and flee.

    C. They left all their tents, gold, clothes, and food behind.

    D. Not only were these lepers fed, but they also became rich and were honored, too, because they were the ones God used to bring the good news to the rest of the city.

    E. How long are you going to sit here—until you die?

    F. Take a step of faith in the direction you believe God wants you to go—do something!

VII. Before you can walk on the water, you have to get out of the boat—you must be willing to depart from what everybody else is doing.

    A. You must be willing to break with tradition, get out there, and run the risk of failure.

    B. Many people are so afraid of failure that they continue to stay in the situation they're in, which guarantees their failure will continue.

    C. If you aren't stretching yourself and believing God for something bigger than what you can produce on your own, you're already a failure.

    D. God is a big God—He is *"able to do exceeding abundantly above all that we ask or think, according to the power that worketh in us"* (Eph. 3:20).

VIII. If your life is "normal" according to the world's system, something is seriously wrong.

    A. There ought to be enough evidence to convict you if you were arrested for being a Christian.

    B. There should be something different about you compared to your unsaved neighbor—they're dead and you're alive!

    C. Before you can see that kind of power manifest in your life, however, you need to make a conscious decision to leave the safety of the boat and get out on the water.

    D. Before you can be a water walker, you must be willing to step out of the boat and run the risk!

TEACHER'S GUIDE

5. People in the boat resist those who are stepping out in faith. It wasn't a sin for the disciples to be in the boat and start out toward the other side. But when our boat encounters a storm—when the doctor says we're going to die—why would we still keep taking their treatment if it's not working? Some people are scared of being different—they have to be like everybody else, yet everybody else is miserable, suffering, and dying. We need to make a decision to be different and just believe God!

5a. People in the boat _____ those stepping out in faith.
    Resist
5b. *Discussion question:* Why do you think people keep taking a treatment if it's not working?
    Discussion question
5c. *Discussion question:* Even though everybody else is miserable, suffering, and dying, why do you think you might still be afraid to be different?
    Discussion question

6. In 2 Kings 7:3-4, Samaria was under siege by the Syrians:

    And there were four leprous men at the entering in of the gate: and they said one to another, Why sit we here until we die? [4] If we say, We will enter into the city, then the famine is in the city, and we shall die there: and if we sit still here, we die also. Now therefore come, and let us fall unto the host of the Syrians: if they save us alive, we shall live; and if they kill us, we shall but die.

These lepers—along with everyone else in the city—were dying of starvation. When the lepers went to the Syrian camp, it turned out that the Lord had caused the Syrians to hear a noise and flee. They left all their tents, gold, clothes, and food behind. Not only were these lepers fed, but they also became rich and were honored, too, because they were the ones God used to bring the good news to the rest of the city. How long are we going to sit here—until we die? Let's take a step of faith in the direction we believe God wants us to go—let's do something!

6a. What did the lepers find when they went to the Syrian camp?
    The Lord has caused the Syrians to hear a noise and flee, leaving behind all their tents, gold, clothes, and food

6b. Not only were these lepers fed, but they also became rich and were _____, too, because they were the ones God used to bring the good news to the rest of the city.
Honored

6c. *Discussion question:* If possible, describe a time when you took a step of faith in the direction God wanted you to go.
Discussion question

7. Before we can walk on the water, we have to get out of the boat—we must be willing to depart from what everybody else is doing. We must be willing to break with tradition, get out there, and run the risk of failure. Many people are so afraid of failure that they continue to stay in the situation they're in, which guarantees their failure will continue. If we aren't stretching ourselves and believing God for something bigger than what we can produce on our own, we're already failures. God is a big God—He is *"able to do exceeding abundantly above all that we ask or think, according to the power that worketh in us"* (Eph. 3:20).

7a. Before you can walk on the water, what must you be willing to do?
   A. Run the risk of failure
   B. Depart from what everybody else is doing
   C. Break with tradition
   D. All of the above
   E. None of the above
   D. All of the above

7b. What can cause people to continue to stay in the situation they're in rather than risk a change?
Fear of failure

7c. *Discussion question:* How is it true that you are already a failure if you don't believe God for something bigger than what you can produce on your own?
Discussion question

8. If our lives are "normal" according to the world's system, something is seriously wrong. There ought to be enough evidence to convict us if we were arrested for being Christians. There should be something different about us compared to our unsaved neighbors—they're dead and we're alive! Before we can see that kind of power manifest in our lives, however, we need to make a conscious decision to leave the safety of the boat and get out on the water. Before we can be water walkers, we must be willing to step out of the boat and run the risk!

8a. True or false: There ought to be enough evidence to convict you if you were arrested for being a Christian.
True

8b. Why should your life be different than your unsaved neighbors'?
They're dead and you're alive

8c. You need to make a _____ to leave the safety of the boat and get out on the water.
Conscious decision

DISCIPLESHIP QUESTIONS

13. People in the boat _____ those stepping out in faith.

14. *Discussion question:* Why do you think people keep taking a treatment if it's not working?

    _____

    _____

    _____

15. *Discussion question:* Even though everybody else is miserable, suffering, and dying, why do you think you might still be afraid to be different?

    _____

    _____

    _____

16. What did the lepers find when they went to the Syrian camp?

    _____

    _____

    _____

17. Not only were these lepers fed, but they also became rich and were _____, too, because they were the ones God used to bring the good news to the rest of the city.

18. *Discussion question:* If possible, describe a time when you took a step of faith in the direction God wanted you to go.

    _____

    _____

    _____

19. Before you can walk on the water, what must you be willing to do?
    A. Run the risk of failure
    B. Depart from what everybody else is doing
    C. Break with tradition
    D. All of the above
    E. None of the above

20. What can cause people to continue to stay in the situation they're in rather than risk a change?

    _____

    _____

    _____

21. *Discussion question:* How is it true that you are already a failure if you don't believe God for something bigger than what you can produce on your own?

    _____

    _____

    _____

22. True or false: There ought to be enough evidence to convict you if you were arrested for being a Christian.

23. Why should your life be different than your unsaved neighbors'?

    _____

    _____

    _____

24. You need to make a _____ to leave the safety of the boat and get out on the water.

Answer Key

13. Resist

14. *Discussion question*

15. *Discussion question*

16. The Lord has caused the Syrians to hear a noise and flee, leaving behind all their tents, gold, clothes, and food

17. Honored

18. *Discussion question*

19. D. All of the above

20. Fear of failure

21. *Discussion question*

22. True

23. They're dead and you're alive

24. Conscious decision

SCRIPTURES

2 KINGS 7:3-4

And there were four leprous men at the entering in of the gate: and they said one to another, Why sit we here until we die? [4] If we say, We will enter into the city, then the famine is in the city, and we shall die there: and if we sit still here, we die also. Now therefore come, and let us fall unto the host of the Syrians: if they save us alive, we shall live; and if they kill us, we shall but die.

EPHESIANS 3:20

Now unto him that is able to do exceeding abundantly above all that we ask or think, according to the power that worketh in us.

TAKE A STEP OF FAITH

LESSON 9

When the Lord touched me on March 23, 1968, He lit a fire in my heart. Even though I had already been born again for ten years, this was when I really got turned on to God. I was in college at the time, and the Lord told me, "Nope, that's not it." God had something bigger for me than being a math major, so He started challenging me to make some decisions.

One of those decisions was to quit school. That meant losing $350 a month in government support from my deceased father's social security. If I stayed in school, I got to keep the money. If I dropped out, I lost it. This caused fear, worry, and concern, because $350 a month for a young single man in 1968 was a decent amount of change. Many people counseled me, saying, "That can't be God. You're taking a huge risk!" So, why did I do it? I wanted to obey the Lord.

Also, this took place at the height of the Vietnam War. I had a school deferment as long as I stayed in college, but if I quit, I could expect an all-expense-paid trip to Vietnam. That was before they had the lottery system for the draft, so it wasn't based on chance. If you quit school and were a healthy eighteen- or nineteen-year-old male, you went to Vietnam. There were no options. I was running the risk of getting hurt, being maimed for life, or even dying. Yet I went ahead and jumped out of the boat!

I took a step out on the water and began walking in the realm of the miraculous. If God didn't come through, I was sunk! Looking back on it now, those were some of the greatest decisions I've ever made in my life. Since then, I've made thousands upon thousands of decisions to step out on the water when it would have been easier to stay in the relative comfort of where I was. But I wanted to believe God. I longed to follow Him and get out where Jesus was.

Since you're reading this book, you probably desire to be out on the water too. You want to be doing something miraculous and making your life count for the kingdom. You long for God's power, but you're afraid to leave the boat.

FAITH KILLERS

Peter would never have walked on the water if he hadn't first stepped out of the boat. You have to get out of the boat before you can walk on water. You can't walk on water in the boat. You have to get out of your comfort zone. The fear of being different, the fear of running a risk, and the desire to be safe are all real faith killers.

Yea, they turned back and tempted God, and limited the Holy One of Israel.

Psalm 78:41

You limit God by not having a vision, fearing the unknown, thinking small, fearing change, being unwilling to take a risk, fearing failure, not taking a step of faith, being lazy, and staying in the boat. Those things limit what God can do in your life. You need to take the limits off God!

OUT ON THE LIMB

Some people just can't transition from taking the so-called security the world has to offer to getting out of the boat. However, the fruit grows out on the limb! Most of us want to hold on to the trunk and still have all the fruit that comes from being out on the limb, but it doesn't work that way. We need to get out where we are bobbing up and down in the breeze. We need to feel the insecurity of wobbling around and wondering, *Is this thing going to hold me or not?* That's where the fruit comes.

When you get out of the boat and start believing God for something big, you will start seeing miracles. For me, it's been nearly four decades of stepping out of the boat, and I get excited every time I do something big! I've taken some big steps in my life. We moved from a small, 14,000-square foot-building to a 110,000-square-foot building. Not only did we take the huge step of buying that building, but we also completed more than $3 million in renovations debt free. While we were doing all of those things, we also doubled our television coverage and more than doubled our staff. That was a huge step out of my boat, and it's not over yet!

I've taken new steps of faith that make those previous steps look small. If the Lord doesn't come through, we're sunk. But I have faith that the best is yet to come. I'll never go back to playing it safe. I'm going for it!

You might say, "Andrew, you shouldn't say that. What happens if it doesn't come to pass?" Well, what happens if it does come to pass? I've seen God come through so many times. I know He's not limited. The only limitation He has is me. So, I'm getting out of the boat!

AFRAID OF FAILURE

So, what if, like Peter, I don't do it perfectly? What happens if I only walk part of the way? What happens if only part of my vision comes to pass? What happens if I shoot at the stars but only hit the moon? Some people would look at that as failure. I look at it as still being better than staying earthbound.

We're just so afraid of failure. We're so scared of what other people say about us. Yet I think the people who are the biggest failures are those who do nothing. If you shoot at nothing and hit it every time, that's failure!

Peter had to get out of the boat. He had to get beyond his immediate circumstances and start believing God for something bigger. If you want to be a water walker, you have to be willing to get out of the boat. Some people refuse to lose sight of the shore. They won't get in over their ankles. They're afraid of what might be out there.

If you knew the water was only six inches deep, you wouldn't mind getting out of the boat. Why? You'd know what's underneath the surface. However, one of the aspects of truly getting out of the boat is not knowing what's out there. You don't know how deep the water is, so you're dealing with the fear of the unknown. You are probably getting in over your head! But in order to get out of the boat and walk on water, you must be willing to trust the results—the future, the unknown—to God.

TRY SOMETHING NEW

You have to be willing to take a risk. If you're the type of person who wants your whole life planned out and simply refuses to take a risk, you'll never walk on water. If you insist on knowing exactly where you'll be, what you'll be doing, and who you will be doing it with twenty years from now, you'll never see God's best. It takes faith to see the real, supernatural power of God.

A good friend of mine says, "God will usually terrify you before He edifies you!" God's vision for your life will be bigger than what you can do, and it will overwhelm you.

My friend also says, "If your dreams and visions don't keep you up at night, you're thinking too small!" If it's God, He'll call you to do something that's beyond your ability. You'll have to get in over your head and run the risk of failure. That just comes with the territory!

Part of being a water walker is being willing to get out of the safety of the boat. You have to depart from what's familiar and what everybody else is doing. You must be willing to try something new. Step out and take a chance!

PARALYZED

One time, I ministered to a man who was paralyzed. He had been paralyzed for twenty years. I prayed for him and he started moving his legs, yet he wouldn't get out of his wheelchair. He always had an excuse—first this, then that. But in my heart, I knew he was healed.

After several weeks of that, he got back to where he was paralyzed again. Finally, he told me, "I'm afraid of getting out of this wheelchair. I've been in it for twenty years. I used to be a sheriff and became paralyzed when I took a bullet to the spine in the line of duty. If I got out of this wheelchair and walked, I would lose my disability checks. Plus, people think I'm a hero. They pity me and sympathize with me. I'd lose that too if I could walk. People would wonder if I was ever really paralyzed. I'm secure. I couldn't go out and get another job now. I don't know how to do anything but be a sheriff, and I'm too old to go back to doing that."

This man was only about fifty years old, but he was afraid to get out of his wheelchair because he became comfortable with the money, sympathy, and attention he received. This guy was paralyzed. He was limited. He was missing out on so much of life but was willing to let it pass him by so he could have money, keep his friends, and have people pity him and sympathize with him. He totally missed the fact that he could have made all kinds of new friends, glorified God, and done things that he hadn't done before. The Lord would have provided for him. Who knows what his future could have been like if he had been willing to get out of that wheelchair?

WHAT IS YOUR BOAT?

That man's wheelchair was his "boat." What is your "boat"? Is your hometown your "boat"? Are you secure in your hometown and afraid to leave? I'm not saying that God tells everyone to leave their hometown, but He may be calling you to do something that would cause you to lose the security of your hometown and some other familiar places. If you were to serve God full force, you might lose some friends. You might say, "But what would I do without them?" Wrong question! What are you not doing because of them? Are you willing to let God's will pass you by just because you're afraid to run the risk and step out of the boat?

I lost some lifelong friends when I made a commitment to serve God. It grieved me at the time, but since then, God has given me millions of other friends—better friends, closer friends. The promise of the hundredfold return is for those who step out of the boat (Mark 10:28-30). Are you going to be one of those who step out of the boat?

It's possible to see what you're leaving, but not what you're missing. In other words, hindsight gives you the ability to look back and see what it cost you to serve God, but you don't have the ability to look forward and see what you'll be missing if you don't serve Him. God is a good God. He'll never require more of you than what He gives to you. You'll always be more blessed following the Lord than you ever would be not following Him. But you must be willing to get out of the boat!

ANDREW'S RECOMMENDATIONS FOR FURTHER STUDY

You need to take the limits off God! My teaching series titled *Don't Limit God* will show you how you can do that.

OUTLINE

I. The Lord lit a fire in my heart and started challenging me to make some decisions.

    A. I took a step out on the water and began walking in the realm of the miraculous; if God didn't come through, I was sunk!

    B. Looking back on it now, those were some of the greatest decisions I've ever made in my life.

    C. It would have been easier to stay in the relative comfort of where I was, but I wanted to believe God.

        i. I longed to follow Him and get out where Jesus was.

II. Peter would never have walked on the water if he hadn't first stepped out of the boat.

    A. You have to get out of your comfort zone.

    B. The fear of being different, the fear of running a risk, and the desire to be safe are all real faith killers.

        Yea, they turned back and tempted God, and limited the Holy One of Israel.

        Psalm 78:41

    C. You limit God by not having a vision, fearing the unknown, thinking small, fearing change, being unwilling to take a risk, fearing failure, not taking a step of faith, being lazy, and staying in the boat.

    D. You need to take the limits off God!

III. The fruit grows out on the limb!

    A. Most of us want to hold on to the trunk and still have all the fruit that comes from being out on the limb, but it doesn't work that way.

    B. We need to get out where we are bobbing up and down in the breeze.

    C. When we get out of the boat and start believing God for something big, we will start seeing miracles.

    D. I have faith that the best is yet to come—I'll never go back to playing it safe.

    E. I'm going for it!

IV. I think the people who are the biggest failures are those who do nothing.

    A. If you shoot at nothing and hit it every time, that's failure!

    B. Peter had to get beyond his immediate circumstances and start believing God for something bigger.

    C. Some people refuse to lose sight of the shore—they won't get in over their ankles.

    D. One of the aspects of truly getting out of the boat is not knowing how deep the water is.

    E. In order to get out of the boat and walk on water, you must be willing to trust the results—the future, the unknown—to God.

V. You have to be willing to take a risk.

    A. If you're the type of person who wants your whole life planned out and simply refuses to take a risk, you'll never walk on water.

    B. If you insist on knowing exactly where you'll be, what you'll be doing, and who you will be doing it with twenty years from now, you'll never see God's best.

    C. It takes faith to see the real, supernatural power of God.

    D. If it's God, He'll call you to do something that's beyond your ability—that just comes with the territory!

VI. God may be calling you to do something that would cause you to lose the security of your hometown and some other familiar places.

    A. If you were to serve God full force, you might lose some friends.

    B. Are you willing to let God's will pass you by just because you're afraid to run the risk?

C. I lost some lifelong friends when I made a commitment to serve God; it grieved me at the time, but since then, God has given me better friends.

    i. The promise of the hundredfold return is for those who step out of the boat (Mark 10:28-30).

D. It's possible to see what you're leaving, but not what you're missing.

E. You'll always be more blessed following the Lord than you ever would be not following Him, but you must be willing to get out of the boat!

ANDREW'S RECOMMENDATIONS FOR FURTHER STUDY

You need to take the limits off God! My teaching series titled *Don't Limit God* will show you how you can do that.

TEACHER'S GUIDE

1. The Lord lit a fire in Andrew's heart and started challenging him to make some decisions. He took a step out on the water and began walking in the realm of the miraculous; if God didn't come through, he was sunk! Looking back on it now, those were some of the greatest decisions he'd ever made in his life. It would have been easier to stay in the relative comfort of where he was, but he wanted to believe God. He longed to follow Him and get out where Jesus was.

1a. True or false: Walking in the realm of the miraculous means that if God doesn't come through, you will sink.
   True
1b. True or false: It is easier to stay in the relative comfort of where you are.
   True
1c. *Discussion question:* What lights a fire in your heart?
   Discussion question
1d. *Discussion question:* What discomfort do you possibly have to overcome to make that desire a reality?
   Discussion question

2. Peter would never have walked on the water if he hadn't first stepped out of the boat. We have to get out of our comfort zones. The fear of being different, the fear of running a risk, and the desire to be safe are all real faith killers.

> *Yea, they turned back and tempted God, and limited the Holy One of Israel.*
>
> Psalm 78:41

We limit God by not having a vision, fearing the unknown, thinking small, fearing change, being unwilling to take a risk, fearing failure, not taking a step of faith, being lazy, and staying in the boat. We need to take the limits off God!

2a. Peter would never have walked on the water if he hadn't first what?
   A. Prayed about it
   B. Fasted
   C. Received approval from the other disciples
   D. Stepped out of the boat
   E. Wrote in his journal
   D. Stepped out of the boat

2b. What are faith killers?

The fear of being different, the fear of running a risk, and the desire to be safe

2c. According to the lesson, what are some ways to limit God?

Not having a vision, fearing the unknown, thinking small, fearing change, being unwilling to take a risk, fearing failure, not taking a step of faith, being lazy, and staying in the boat

2d. *Discussion question:* How do you think you limit God in your life?

Discussion question

3. The fruit grows out on the limb! Most of us want to hold on to the trunk and still have all the fruit that comes from being out on the limb, but it doesn't work that way. We need to get out where we are bobbing up and down in the breeze. When we get out of the boat and start believing God for something big, we will start seeing miracles. Andrew has faith that the best is yet to come—he'll never go back to playing it safe. He's going for it!

3a. The fruit grows out on the _____!
   A. Roots
   B. Trunk
   C. Other fruit
   D. Leaves
   E. Limb
   E. Limb

3b. What happens when you get out of the boat and start believing God for something big?

You will start seeing miracles

3c. *Discussion question:* What steps do you need to take to get out of your boat?

Discussion question

4. Andrew thinks the people who are the biggest failures are those who do nothing. If we shoot at nothing and hit it every time, that's failure! Peter had to get beyond his immediate circumstances and start believing God for something bigger. Some people refuse to lose sight of the shore—they won't get in over their ankles. One of the aspects of truly getting out of the boat is not knowing how deep the water is. In order to get out of the boat and walk on water, we must be willing to trust the results—the future, the unknown—to God.

4a. Who are the biggest failures?
   A. Those who do nothing
   B. Those who make mistakes
   C. Those who don't succeed
   D. Those who go halfway
   E. Those who don't do enough
   A. Those who do nothing

4b. What did Peter have to get beyond to start believing God for something bigger?
   His immediate circumstances

4c. What must you be willing to trust God with in order to get out of the boat?
   The results, the future, the unknown

4d. *Discussion question:* To step out of your boat, what must you personally need to trust God with?
   Discussion question

5. We have to be willing to take a risk. If we're the type of people who want our whole lives planned out and simply refuse to take a risk, we'll never walk on water. If we insist on knowing exactly where we'll be, what we'll be doing, and who we will be doing it with twenty years from now, we'll never see God's best. It takes faith to see the real, supernatural power of God. If it's God, He'll call us to do something that's beyond our ability—that just comes with the territory!

5a. You'll never walk on water if what?
   If you want your whole life planned out and simply refuse to take a risk

5b. What does it take to see the real, supernatural power of God?
   Faith

5c. True or false: If it's God, He'll call you to do something that's beyond your ability.
   True

5d. *Discussion question:* What are you insistent on knowing about your life that you need to give to God?
   Discussion question

6. God may be calling us to do something that would cause us to lose the security of our hometown and some other familiar places. If we were to serve God full force, we might lose some friends. Are we willing to let God's will pass us by just because we're afraid to run the risk? Andrew lost some lifelong friends when he made a commitment to serve God; it grieved him at the time, but since then, God has given him better friends. The promise of the hundredfold return is for those who step out of the boat (Mark 10:28-30). It is possible to see what we're leaving, but not what we're missing.

We'll always be more blessed following the Lord than we ever would be not following Him, but we must be willing to get out of the boat!

6a. God may be calling you to do something that would cause you to lose what?
   A. Peace
   B. Hope
   C. Joy
   D. Security
   E. Vision
   D. Security

6b. Who is promised the hundredfold return (Mark 10:28-30)?
   Those who step out of the boat

6c. *Discussion question:* What do you find security in other than God?
   Discussion question

6d. *Discussion question:* By not giving up your security, what do you think you may be missing out on?
   Discussion question

DISCIPLESHIP QUESTIONS

1. True or false: Walking in the realm of the miraculous means that if God doesn't come through, you will sink.

2. True or false: It is easier to stay in the relative comfort of where you are.

3. *Discussion question:* What lights a fire in your heart?

    _____

    _____

    _____

4. *Discussion question:* What discomfort do you possibly have to overcome to make that desire a reality?

    _____

    _____

    _____

5. Peter would never have walked on the water if he hadn't first what?
    A. Prayed about it
    B. Fasted
    C. Received approval from the other disciples
    D. Stepped out of the boat
    E. Wrote in his journal

6. What are faith killers?

    _____

    _____

    _____

7. According to the lesson, what are some ways to limit God?

    _____

    _____

    _____

8. *Discussion question:* How do you think you limit God in your life?

    _____

    _____

    _____

9. The fruit grows out on the _____!
    A. Roots
    B. Trunk
    C. Other fruit
    D. Leaves
    E. Limb

10. What happens when you get out of the boat and start believing God for something big?

    _____

    _____

    _____

11. *Discussion question:* What steps do you need to take to get out of your boat?

    _____

    _____

    _____

12. Who are the biggest failures?
    A. Those who do nothing
    B. Those who make mistakes
    C. Those who don't succeed
    D. Those who go halfway
    E. Those who don't do enough

13. What did Peter have to get beyond to start believing God for something bigger?

_____

_____

_____

14. What must you be willing to trust God with in order to get out of the boat?

_____

_____

_____

15. _Discussion question:_ To step out of your boat, what must you personally need to trust God with?

_____

_____

_____

16. You'll never walk on water if what?

_____

_____

_____

17. What does it take to see the real, supernatural power of God?

_____

_____

_____

18. True or false: If it's God, He'll call you to do something that's beyond your ability.

19. *Discussion question:* What are you insistent on knowing about your life that you need to give to God?

_____

_____

_____

20. God may be calling you to do something that would cause you to lose what?
    A. Peace
    B. Hope
    C. Joy
    D. Security
    E. Vision

21. Who is promised the hundredfold return (Mark 10:28-30)?

_____

_____

_____

22. *Discussion question:* What do you find security in other than God?

_____

_____

_____

23. *Discussion question:* By not giving up your security, what do you think you may be missing out on?

_____

_____

_____

ANSWER KEY

1. True

2. True

3. *Discussion question*

4. *Discussion question*

5. D. Stepped out of the boat

6. The fear of being different, the fear of running a risk, and the desire to be safe

7. Not having a vision, fearing the unknown, thinking small, fearing change, being unwilling to take a risk, fearing failure, not taking a step of faith, being lazy, and staying in the boat

8. *Discussion question*

9. E. Limb

10. You will start seeing miracles

11. *Discussion question*

12. A. Those who do nothing

13. His immediate circumstances

14. The results, the future, the unknown

15. *Discussion question*

16. If you want your whole life planned out and simply refuse to take a risk

17. Faith

18. True

19. *Discussion question*

20. D. Security

21. Those who step out of the boat

22. *Discussion question*

23. *Discussion question*

Scriptures

PSALM 78:41

Yea, they turned back and tempted God, and limited the Holy One of Israel.

MARK 10:28-30

Then Peter began to say unto him, Lo, we have left all, and have
followed thee. [29] And Jesus answered and said, Verily I say unto you,
There is no man that hath left house, or brethren, or sisters, or father,
or mother, or wife, or children, or lands, for my sake, and the gospel's,
[30] But he shall receive an hundredfold now in this time, houses,
and brethren, and sisters, and mothers, and children, and lands, with
persecutions; and in the world to come eternal life.

FAITH PLEASES GOD

LESSON 10

Peter walked on the water, and people criticized him. However, outside of Jesus himself, he's the only person who has ever physically walked on water. Peter may not have done it perfectly, but he did it. I believe God was thrilled when Peter stepped out of the boat and walked on the water, I really do.

> *But without faith it is impossible to please him: for he that cometh to God must believe that he is, and that he is a rewarder of them that diligently seek him*
>
> Hebrews 11:6

There have been times when I've failed. I've started trying to believe God and made some mistakes. After going two steps forward, I've had to retreat and take one step back. I've had to lay off staff and cancel radio stations. I've had to back up at times. I don't think it was God's will. I just didn't do it perfectly. I've stumbled and fallen along the way. There have been times when I was late paying my bills. That's not the way the Lord wanted it to be. Praise God, I haven't been late on a bill since the early 1990s.

There was a time in my ministry when we struggled. There was a time when I failed and didn't represent God accurately. People criticized me and said, "Some Christian you are!" Some people focused on the fact that I didn't do things perfectly and condemned me. But I believe God was looking at me and saying, "He might not be doing it exactly right yet, but at least he has stepped out of the boat and is trying!"

I don't think the Lord would fault me or come against me for trying to obey Him. I haven't always done things correctly. Sometimes I've taken a word and made a paragraph out of it. Some people have looked at that and said, "So, you were just all wrong!" Well, yeah, I've missed it and made mistakes—but God loves faith! Without faith, it's impossible to please Him (Heb. 11:6). Faith is what pleases God. Even though I may have failed at times, the Lord just encouraged me and urged me on!

I remember when my kids were learning how to ride a bicycle. It took a few tries before they really got the hang of it. They made some mistakes along the way. It would have been wonderful if they had just gotten on a bicycle and ridden it perfectly—never wobbling and doing everything right on the first try—but most children don't do that. Due to fear, most of them wobble, fall, and maybe even hurt themselves. But their father gets them up, encourages them, and says, "You can do it! It's not that bad. I fell off my bike when I was learning to ride also."

As a loving parent, you just encourage your children to keep at it until, eventually, they master the skill of riding a bike. All along the way, you just look at them and encourage them, saying, "I'm proud of you for trying!"

Our heavenly Father is more like this than we suspect. When Peter began to sink, instead of God saying, "You didn't do it perfectly. You failed. You didn't walk all the way to Jesus. You only got twenty yards!" I believe He exclaimed, "Peter actually walked on water!" Peter did something that no other human being besides Jesus had ever done. I believe God was impressed! He was thrilled to see His son out there trying! Even though Peter failed and started to sink, God was pleased.

GET UP AND TRY AGAIN

You may fail. When you get out of the boat, you run the risk of sinking. Peter didn't go all the way under the water. But he began to sink (Matt. 14:30), and Jesus had to rescue him. The good news is that God delivered Peter; He didn't just push him down under the water, saying, "You sorry thing. Your faith failed! You didn't keep believing Me. How dare you!" No! Instead of letting him sink, the Lord reached out and lifted him up by his hand.

If you fail, Jesus will be there. Even though people may be hard on you and say "Well, you didn't do things right," Jesus will encourage you to keep trying. He'll say, "I'm so proud of you. Go for it! Get up and try again!"

If you want to walk on water, you have to get out of the boat. You have to do something. If you fail, the Lord won't fall off of His throne. The kingdom of God isn't going to totally rise or fall based on your success or failure. If you fail at believing God, you're still a success. You tried. You got out of the boat. You walked on water.

If you're doing it out of your own presumption, because you aren't waiting on God, His way, and His timing—that's a different situation. But if you're doing it out of a pure heart and can truthfully say, "Father, I'm doing this because I believe with all my heart that this is You leading me to take a step of faith, trust You, get out of this boat, and move in this direction," then go for it! If you fail, you won't be a failure. You'll be a success in God's eyes!

FOLLOW HIS LEADING

When we stand before God and He judges us for what happened in our lifetime, I believe we'll be surprised. He's going to look at some people whom the world considered failures and say, "You stepped out in faith and were trying to obey Me." Faith is what pleases God!

The Lord is more pleased with faith than He is with "success." If you could somehow or another "succeed" without trusting God, you've failed. You could have money, prestige, honor, recognition, possessions, and influence, but if you haven't really trusted God and stepped out to do what He wanted you to do, you've failed. You might be considered a great success in the eyes of others, but God will look at you and say, "You failed to do what I told you to do."

On the other hand, there will be people who didn't amount to much in the eyes of the world. They didn't have much, yet they trusted God. They believed Him and did what He told them to do. The Lord will say to them, "You good and faithful servant!" God never bases His opinion of faithfulness only on the outcome but, rather, on whether or not we were following His leading. That's encouraging!

If we want to walk on water and see the miracle power of God manifest in our lives, we need to get out of the boat and trust God. If we fail, we've learned something. Jesus will pick us up. And if the Lord tarries, someday 2,000 years in the future, people will be talking about how we trusted God. We'll be an inspiration to somebody else the way Peter is to us. If Peter had stayed in the boat, we wouldn't be discussing him walking on water. That chapter in the Bible wouldn't be there. Praise God that somebody had enough faith to trust God. Although he failed, I admire Peter for being able to look beyond himself, get out of the boat, step out there on the water, and trust Jesus. That's awesome!

Do you want to walk on the water? Make a break! Get out of the boat! Do something!

OUTLINE

I. Peter may not have done it perfectly, but I believe God was thrilled when Peter stepped out of the boat and walked on the water.

    A. There have been times when I've started trying to believe God and made so many mistakes.

    B. I've stumbled and fallen along the way.

    C. I don't think the Lord would fault me or come against me for trying to obey Him.

    D. I've missed it and made mistakes—but God loves faith!

       But without faith it is impossible to please him: for he that cometh to God must believe that he is, and that he is a rewarder of them that diligently seek him.

                                             Hebrews 11:6

    E. Even though I may have failed at times, the Lord just encouraged me and urged me on!

II. You may fail.

    A. When you get out of the boat, you run the risk of sinking.

    B. Peter didn't go all the way under the water; but he began to sink (Matt. 14:30), and Jesus had to rescue him.

    C. If you fail, Jesus will be there—He will encourage you to keep trying.

        i. The kingdom of God isn't going to totally rise or fall based on your success or failure.

    D. If you fail at believing God, you're still a success: You tried.

    E. If you're doing it out of your own presumption, because you aren't waiting on God, His way, and His timing—that's a different situation.

    F. But if you're doing it out of a pure heart, then go for it!

III. Faith is what pleases God!

    A. If we could somehow or another "succeed" without trusting God, we've failed.

    B. We might be considered a great success in the eyes of others, but God will look at us and say, "You failed to do what I told you to do."

    C. God never bases His opinion of faithfulness only on the outcome but, rather, on whether or not we were following His leading.

    D. Although Peter failed, I admire him for being able to look beyond himself, get out of the boat, step out on the water, and trust Jesus.

TEACHER'S GUIDE

1. Peter may not have done it perfectly, but Andrew believes God was thrilled when Peter stepped out of the boat and walked on the water. There have been times when Andrew has started trying to believe God and made some mistakes. He's stumbled and fallen along the way. He doesn't think the Lord would fault him or come against him for trying to obey Him. Andrew has missed it and made mistakes—but God loves faith!

> *But without faith it is impossible to please him: for he that cometh to God must believe that he is, and that he is a rewarder of them that diligently seek him.*
>
> Hebrews 11:6

Even though Andrew may have failed at times, the Lord just encouraged him and urged him on!

1a. What does God love (Heb. 11:6)?
   Faith
1b. Even though Andrew may have failed at times, the Lord just _____ him and _____ him on!
   Encouraged / urged
1c. *Discussion question:* Share a time in your life when you made a mistake and how God encouraged you.
   Discussion question

2. We may fail. When we get out of the boat, we run the risk of sinking. Peter didn't go all the way under the water; but he began to sink (Matt. 14:30), and Jesus had to rescue him. If we fail, Jesus will be there—He will encourage us to keep trying. The kingdom of God isn't going to totally rise or fall based on our success or failure. If we fail at believing God, we're still a success: We tried. If we're doing it out of our own presumption, because we aren't waiting on God, His way, and His timing—that's a different situation. But if we're doing it out of a pure heart, then we should go for it!

2a. What happens when you get out of the boat?
   You run the risk of sinking
2b. True or false: If you fail, you're all on your own.
   False
2c. *Discussion question:* What difference does your heart attitude make regarding your success or failure?
   Discussion question

3. Faith is what pleases God! If we could somehow or another "succeed" without trusting God, we've failed. We might be considered a great success in the eyes of others, but God will look at us and say, "You failed to do what I told you to do." God never bases His opinion of faithfulness only on the outcome but, rather, on whether or not we were following His leading. Although Peter failed, Andrew admires him for being able to look beyond himself, get out of the boat, step out on the water, and trust Jesus.

3a. If you could somehow or another _____ without trusting God,
    you've _____.
    "Succeed" / failed

3b. *Discussion question:* Why does it not matter if you are a great success in the eyes
    of others?
    Discussion question

3c. True or false: God never bases His opinion of faithfulness only on the outcome.
    True

3d. What does God base His opinion of faithfulness on?
    A. What Andrew says
    B. Whether or not you were following His leading
    C. Whether or not you meant well
    D. The majority vote
    E. Whether or not you've read your Bible and paid your tithe
    B. Whether or not you were following His leading

3e. *Discussion question:* Why can Peter be admired today, even though he failed?
    Discussion question

DISCIPLESHIP QUESTIONS

1. What does God love (Heb. 11:6)?

    _____

    _____

    _____

2. Even though Andrew may have failed at times, the Lord just _____ him and _____ him on!

3. *Discussion question:* Share a time in your life when you made a mistake and how God encouraged you.

    _____

    _____

    _____

4. What happens when you get out of the boat?

    _____

    _____

    _____

5. True or false: If you fail, you're all on your own.

6. *Discussion question:* What difference does your heart attitude make regarding your success or failure?

    _____

    _____

    _____

7. If you could somehow or another _____ without trusting God, you've _____.

8.   *Discussion question:* Why does it not matter if you are a great success in the eyes of others?

_____

_____

_____

9.   True or false: God never bases His opinion of faithfulness only on the outcome.

10. What does God base His opinion of faithfulness on?
     A.   What Andrew says
     B.   Whether or not you were following His leading
     C.   Whether or not you meant well
     D.   The majority vote
     E.   Whether or not you've read your Bible and paid your tithe

11. *Discussion question:* Why can Peter be admired today, even though he failed?

_____

_____

_____

ANSWER KEY

1. Faith

2. Encouraged / urged

3. *Discussion question*

4. You run the risk of sinking

5. False

6. *Discussion question*

7. "Succeed" / failed

8. *Discussion question*

9. True

10. B. Whether or not you were following His leading

11. *Discussion question*

SCRIPTURES

HEBREWS 11:6

But without faith it is impossible to please him: for he that cometh
to God must believe that he is, and that he is a rewarder of them that
diligently seek him.

MATTHEW 14:30

But when he saw the wind boisterous, he was afraid; and beginning to
sink, he cried, saying, Lord, save me.

BECAUSE OF YOUR UNBELIEF

LESSON 11

And when Peter was come down out of the ship, he walked on the water, to go to Jesus.

Matthew 14:29

In order to walk on water, you have to get out of the boat. You must leave the comfort and security of whatever you're in and take a risk. Depart from the norm. Separate yourself from the crowd. Do something! Everybody wants to walk on water, but nobody wants to get out of the boat.

But when he [Peter] saw the wind boisterous, he was afraid; and beginning to sink, he cried, saying, Lord, save me. [31] And immediately Jesus stretched forth his hand, and caught him, and said unto him, O thou of little faith, wherefore didst thou doubt? [32] And when they were come into the ship, the wind ceased. [33] Then they that were in the ship came and worshipped him, saying, Of a truth, thou art the Son of God.

Matthew 14:30-33, brackets mine

And the sea arose by reason of a great wind that blew. [19] So when they had rowed about five and twenty or thirty furlongs, they see Jesus walking on the sea, and drawing nigh unto the ship: and they were afraid. [20] But he saith unto them, It is I; be not afraid. [21] Then they willingly received him into the ship: and immediately the ship was at the land whither they went.

John 6:18-21

This is one reason we need to take all of the Gospels' accounts of one story and put them together. Only Matthew shows Peter making this request of Jesus and walking on the water. Only John records that when Jesus entered into the ship, not only did the wind cease, but also the ship and all of its occupants were immediately translated to the other shore. Mark recounts some things Jesus said about hardness of heart. If we just had Mark's account, we wouldn't know that Peter walked on the water and that the boat was translated with the occupants to the other shore. Even though the events still would have been miraculous, we would have missed some of the information. We get a little different slant from each Gospel. In order to get the full story, we need to put them all together.

THE NATURAL REALM

Peter got out of the boat and walked on the water. But Matthew 14:30 specifically says,

> But when he saw the wind boisterous, he was afraid; and beginning to sink, he cried, saying, Lord, save me.

Peter saw the boisterous wind, was afraid, and started to sink. What did the wind being boisterous have to do with Peter walking on the water? The thing (in this case, the wind) that took his attention away from Jesus and caused him to begin to sink was a non-factor. It really didn't have anything to do with it. If Peter had kept his eyes on Jesus, the Author and Finisher of his faith (Heb. 12:2), he would have walked on water all the way to the Lord. Then he could have walked with Jesus back to the boat, or the shore, or anywhere else he wanted to go. He had already proven that he could walk on water. He had already defied the laws of nature. He was walking by faith. The wind and the waves didn't have anything to do with him walking on the water. In the natural, he couldn't have walked on the water if it had been a perfectly calm day. The wind was just something that took his attention away from Jesus.

When Peter took his eyes off Jesus and began to look at the wind and the waves, he started focusing on the natural realm. Then the natural realm probably began to flood his senses with thoughts like, *You shouldn't be here. This is crazy. You can't do this.* We've all been taught not to get out on a lake and try to walk on water. Peter had also spent his whole life learning that it's better to stay in the boat, so when he saw the wind and the waves, it brought all those things back to his remembrance and caused him to doubt.

"LITTLE FAITH"

When Peter cried out *"Lord, save me,"* Jesus immediately *"stretched forth his hand, and caught him, and said unto him, O thou of little faith, wherefore didst thou doubt?"* (Matt. 14:31).

Notice how Jesus said that Peter had *"little faith."* Most people believe that to do something really miraculous, they have to have big faith, great faith, or tons of faith. But the Lord said Peter had little faith. Yet as long as that little faith was focused on Jesus, it was enough to walk on water.

> *O thou of little faith, wherefore didst thou doubt?*
>
> Matthew 14:31b

Jesus brought up an important truth here that most Christians haven't really understood, because they're too busy trying to build their faith and come up with a "big" faith. However, the key to the Christian life isn't "big" faith but, rather, "little" unbelief.

MEET THE PEOPLE'S NEEDS

When Jesus and three of His disciples came down from the Mount of Transfiguration, there was a man who had brought his demonized son to Jesus to cast the demon out. Since the Lord was up on the mountain with Peter, James, and John, the man asked the other disciples to cast the demon out. They tried, but couldn't.

> *And when they* [Jesus and the three disciples returning with Him] *were come to the multitude, there came to him a certain man, kneeling down to him, and saying,* [15] *Lord, have mercy on my son: for he is lunatick, and sore vexed: for ofttimes he falleth into the fire, and oft into the water.*
>
> Matthew 17:14-15, brackets mine

The word *"lunatick"* means that the boy had some type of seizure. While convulsing the boy, the demon would throw him into the fire and into the water. Most scholars believe this refers to something like epilepsy.

> *And I brought him to thy disciples, and they could not cure him.* [17] *Then Jesus answered and said, O faithless and perverse generation, how long shall I be with you? how long shall I suffer you? bring him hither to me.*
>
> Matthew 17:16-17

Jesus didn't say, "Guys, I'm sorry. This isn't your responsibility. You don't have the power to deal with this. I should have been here for you. Don't feel bad about it." Not at all! Instead, the Lord replied, *"O faithless and perverse generation"* (Matt. 17:17).

He rebuked them, basically saying, "How long am I going to be here?" In other words, Jesus wanted His disciples to be able to carry on His ministry.

Today the church doesn't feel any conviction about not meeting the needs of society. We send people who come to us with mental problems to a psychiatrist or a mental ward. We send people with sickness to a doctor. We send people with financial problems to a banker or to the government for welfare. However, God intended for the church to meet the physical, social, and emotional needs of people. God is not pleased today with the church's inability to do this. If Jesus were here in His physical body, He would be saying the same basic thing: "You're supposed to be healing the sick, cleansing the lepers, and raising the dead. You don't have to send people to psychiatrists and welfare. You ought to be meeting the needs of people!"

WHY DIDN'T IT WORK?

And Jesus rebuked the devil; and he departed out of him: and the child was cured from that very hour. [19] Then came the disciples to Jesus apart, and said, Why could not we cast him out?

Matthew 17:18-19

Now, the disciples asked a very important question. In Matthew 10, the disciples received a commission from the Lord. He gave them authority and power over all unclean spirits, to cast them out. The disciples went out, came back, and didn't ask any questions like "Why didn't it work?" or "How come this didn't happen?" The absence of questions implies that they'd seen 100 percent success. But in Matthew 17, they did the same thing they had done before, but without the same results.

Have you ever prayed for something that you really believed was God's will, but didn't see it come to pass? Perhaps you've seen yourself or someone else healed or set free before, but this time it didn't manifest. Due to that, you have a specific quandary, because you know what you believe. You've seen faith work before, but this time you did everything you knew to do as far as you could tell, but didn't get the right results.

It's significant to point this out, because there are some people who just don't believe that God does miracles today. Those people aren't asking "Why didn't it work when I prayed?" because they didn't expect God to move. The believers who are the most upset and susceptible to condemnation or feelings that God failed them are those who know that faith works, have believed, or have seen others set free. Yet they did the same thing this time as before and didn't see anything come to pass.

Therefore, the disciples' question—and Jesus' answer—are both very important.

Jesus said unto them, Because of your unbelief.

Matthew 17:20a

Jesus didn't say that it was because they didn't believe or because of their "little faith" (as the *New International Version* and others incorrectly translated it). That's what most people believe. They think, *Well, wait a minute. If the disciples prayed for something and didn't see it come to pass, it's because they didn't have any faith or their faith was too small.* That's not what Jesus said. It's possible to believe and yet have unbelief at the same time.

OUTLINE

I.   This is one reason we need to take all of the Gospels' accounts of one story and put them together—

> *And when Peter was come down out of the ship, he walked on the water, to go to Jesus. [30] But when he [Peter] saw the wind boisterous, he was afraid; and beginning to sink, he cried, saying, Lord, save me. [31] And immediately Jesus stretched forth his hand, and caught him, and said unto him, O thou of little faith, wherefore didst thou doubt? [32] And when they were come into the ship, the wind ceased. [33] Then they that were in the ship came and worshipped him, saying, Of a truth, thou art the Son of God.*
>
> Matthew 14:29-33, brackets mine

> *And the sea arose by reason of a great wind that blew. [19] So when they had rowed about five and twenty or thirty furlongs, they see Jesus walking on the sea, and drawing nigh unto the ship: and they were afraid. [20] But he saith unto them, It is I; be not afraid. [21] Then they willingly received him into the ship: and immediately the ship was at the land whither they went.*
>
> John 6:18-21

A.   Only Matthew shows Peter making this request of Jesus and walking on the water.

B.   Only John records that when Jesus entered into the ship, not only did the wind cease, but also the ship and all of its occupants were immediately translated to the other shore.

C.   Mark recounts some things Jesus said about hardness of heart; if we just had Mark's account, we wouldn't know that Peter walked on the water and that the boat was translated with the occupants to the other shore.

D.   Even though the events still would have been miraculous, we would have missed some of the information.

E.   We get a little different slant from each Gospel; in order to get the full story, we need to put them all together.

II.   Peter got out of the boat and walked on the water, but Matthew 14:30 specifically says,

But when he saw the wind boisterous, he was afraid; and beginning to sink, he cried, saying, Lord, save me.

A. The wind that took his attention away from Jesus and caused him to begin to sink was a non-factor.

B. In the natural, he couldn't have walked on the water if it had been a perfectly calm day.

C. When Peter took his eyes off Jesus and began to look at the wind and the waves, he started focusing on the natural realm; then the natural realm probably began to flood his senses.

D. Peter had spent his whole life learning that it's better to stay in the boat, so when he saw the wind and the waves, it brought all those things back to his remembrance and caused him to doubt.

III. When Peter cried out *"Lord, save me,"* Jesus immediately *"stretched forth his hand, and caught him, and said unto him, O thou of little faith, wherefore didst thou doubt"* (Matt. 14:31).

A. Notice how Jesus said that Peter had *"little faith."*

B. Most people believe that to do something really miraculous, they have to have big faith, great faith, or tons of faith, but the Lord said Peter had little faith.

C. As long as that little faith was focused on Jesus, it was enough to walk on water.

D. The key to the Christian life isn't "big" faith but, rather, "little" unbelief.

IV. When Jesus and three of His disciples came down from the Mount of Transfiguration, there was a man who had brought his demonized son to Jesus to cast the demon out.

A. Since the Lord was up on the mountain with Peter, James, and John, the man asked the other disciples to cast the demon out; they tried, but couldn't.

And when they [Jesus and the three disciples returning with Him] *were come to the multitude, there came to him a certain man, kneeling down to him, and saying,* [15] *Lord, have mercy on my son: for he is lunatick, and sore vexed: for ofttimes he falleth into the fire, and oft into the water.*

Matthew 17:14-15, brackets mine

    i.   The word *"lunatick"* means that the boy had some type of seizure—while convulsing the boy, the demon would throw him into the fire and into the water.

B. Jesus didn't say, "I'm sorry. This isn't your responsibility. You don't have the power to deal with this. I should have been here for you. Don't feel bad about it."

C. Instead, the Lord replied, *"O faithless and perverse generation"* (Matt. 17:17).

D. He rebuked them, basically saying, "How long am I going to be here?"

E. Jesus wanted His disciples to be able to carry on His ministry.

F. Today Jesus would be saying the same thing: "You're supposed to be healing the sick, cleansing the lepers, and raising the dead. You don't have to send people to psychiatrists and welfare. You ought to be meeting the needs of people!"

V. The disciples asked a very important question—

And Jesus rebuked the devil; and he departed out of him: and the child was cured from that very hour. [19] *Then came the disciples to Jesus apart, and said, Why could not we cast him out?*

Matthew 17:18-19

A. In Matthew 10, the disciples received a commission from the Lord, went out, came back, and didn't ask any questions like "Why didn't it work?"

    i.   The absence of questions implies that they'd seen 100 percent success.

B. But in Matthew 17, they did the same thing they had done before, but without the same results.

C. Have you ever prayed for something that you really believed was God's will, but didn't see it come to pass?

D. Some people just don't believe that God does miracles today; those people aren't asking "Why didn't it work when I prayed?" because they didn't expect God to move.

E. The believers who are the most upset and susceptible to condemnation or feelings that God failed them are those who know that faith works, have believed, or have seen others set free; yet they did the same thing this time as before and didn't see anything come to pass.

F. Therefore, the disciples' question—and Jesus' answer—are both very important:

Jesus said unto them, Because of your unbelief.
Matthew 17:20a

i. Jesus didn't say that it was because they didn't believe or because of their "little faith" (as the *New International Version* and others incorrectly translated it); that's what most people believe.

ii. It's possible to believe and yet have unbelief at the same time.

TEACHER'S GUIDE

1. This is one reason we need to take all of the Gospels' accounts of one story and put them together—

> *And when Peter was come down out of the ship, he walked on the water, to go to Jesus.* [30] *But when he* [Peter] *saw the wind boisterous, he was afraid; and beginning to sink, he cried, saying, Lord, save me.* [31] *And immediately Jesus stretched forth his hand, and caught him, and said unto him, O thou of little faith, wherefore didst thou doubt?* [32] *And when they were come into the ship, the wind ceased.* [33] *Then they that were in the ship came and worshipped him, saying, Of a truth, thou art the Son of God.*
>
> Matthew 14:29-33, brackets mine

> *And the sea arose by reason of a great wind that blew.* [19] *So when they had rowed about five and twenty or thirty furlongs, they see Jesus walking on the sea, and drawing nigh unto the ship: and they were afraid.* [20] *But he saith unto them, It is I; be not afraid.* [21] *Then they willingly received him into the ship: and immediately the ship was at the land whither they went.*
>
> John 6:18-21

Only Matthew shows Peter making this request of Jesus and walking on the water. Only John records that when Jesus entered into the ship, not only did the wind cease, but also the ship and all of its occupants were immediately translated to the other shore. Mark recounts some things Jesus said about hardness of heart; if we just had Mark's account, we wouldn't know that Peter walked on the water and that the boat was translated with the occupants to the other shore. Even though the events still would have been miraculous, we would have missed some of the information. We get a little different slant from each Gospel; in order to get the full story, we need to put them all together.

1a. Only Matthew shows Peter doing what?
   Making this request of Jesus and walking on the water
1b. According to the Gospel of John, what happened when Jesus entered into the ship?
   The wind ceased, and the ship and all of its occupants were immediately translated to the other shore
1c. Mark recounts some things Jesus said about what?
   Hardness of heart
1d. *Discussion question:* What other Bible stories need all four Gospel accounts of them to paint a whole picture?
   Discussion question

2. Peter got out of the boat and walked on the water, but Matthew 14:30 specifically says,

> *But when he saw the wind boisterous, he was afraid; and beginning to sink, he cried, saying, Lord, save me.*

The wind that took his attention away from Jesus and caused him to begin to sink was a non-factor. In the natural, he couldn't have walked on the water if it had been a perfectly calm day. When Peter took his eyes off Jesus and began to look at the wind and the waves, he started focusing on the natural realm; then the natural realm probably began to flood his senses. Peter had spent his whole life learning that it's better to stay in the boat, so when he saw the wind and the waves, it brought all those things back to his remembrance and caused him to doubt.

2a. When Peter took his eyes off Jesus and looked at the wind and waves, what did he start to do?
    He started focusing on the natural realm
2b. Peter had spent his whole life learning that it's better to do what?
    A. Walk on water
    B. Fly
    C. Multitask
    D. Stay in the boat
    E. Talk to strangers
    D. Stay in the boat
2c. *Discussion question:* What have you learned to do all of your life that keeps you from stepping out?
    Discussion question

3. When Peter cried out *"Lord, save me,"* Jesus immediately *"stretched forth his hand, and caught him, and said unto him, O thou of little faith, wherefore didst thou doubt?"* (Matt. 14:31). We need to take notice of how Jesus said that Peter had *"little faith."* Most people believe that to do something really miraculous, they have to have big faith, great faith, or tons of faith, but the Lord said Peter had little faith. As long as that little faith was focused on Jesus, it was enough to walk on water. However, the key to the Christian life isn't "big" faith but, rather, "little" unbelief.

3a. Jesus said that Peter had _____.
    A. Weak faith
    B. Little faith
    C. No faith
    D. Strong faith
    E. A lot of faith

B. Little faith

3b. True or false: Little faith focused on Jesus is enough to walk on water.

True

3c. The key to the Christian life is_____.

    A. Little unbelief
    B. Big faith
    C. Strong faith
    D. No faith
    E. Little belief

A. Little unbelief

3d. *Discussion question:* What is the difference between little faith and unbelief?

Discussion question

4. When Jesus and three of His disciples came down from the Mount of Transfiguration, there was a man who had brought his demonized son to Jesus to cast the demon out. Since the Lord was up on the mountain with Peter, James, and John, the man asked the other disciples to cast the demon out; they tried, but couldn't.

> *And when they* [Jesus and the three disciples returning with Him] *were come to the multitude, there came to him a certain man, kneeling down to him, and saying,* [15] *Lord, have mercy on my son: for he is lunatick, and sore vexed: for ofttimes he falleth into the fire, and oft into the water.*
>
> Matthew 17:14-15, brackets mine

The word *"lunatick"* means that the boy had some type of seizure—while convulsing the boy, the demon would throw him into the fire and into the water. Jesus didn't say, "I'm sorry. This isn't your responsibility. You don't have the power to deal with this. I should have been here for you. Don't feel bad about it." Instead, the Lord replied, *"O faithless and perverse generation"* (Matt. 17:17). He rebuked them, basically saying, "How long am I going to be here?" Jesus wanted His disciples to be able to carry on His ministry. Today Jesus would be saying the same thing: "You're supposed to be healing the sick, cleansing the lepers, and raising the dead. You don't have to send people to psychiatrists and welfare. You ought to be meeting the needs of people!"

4a. The word *"lunatick"* means that the boy had some type of _____.

Seizure

4b. What was Jesus' reply when he found out the disciples could not cast the demon out?

"O faithless and perverse generation"

4c. *Discussion question:* What needs can you supernaturally or naturally meet for the people in your life?

Discussion question

5. The disciples asked a very important question—

And Jesus rebuked the devil; and he departed out of him: and the child was cured from that very hour. [19] Then came the disciples to Jesus apart, and said, Why could not we cast him out?

Matthew 17:18-19

In Matthew 10, the disciples received a commission from the Lord, went out, came back, and didn't ask any questions like "Why didn't it work?" The absence of questions implies that they'd seen 100 percent success. But in Matthew 17, they did the same thing they had done before, but without the same results. At times, we pray for something that we really believe is God's will, but don't see it come to pass. Some people just don't believe that God does miracles today; those people aren't asking "Why didn't it work when I prayed?" because they didn't expect God to move. The believers who are the most upset and susceptible to condemnation or feelings that God failed them are those who know that faith works, have believed, or have seen others set free; yet they did the same thing this time and didn't see anything come to pass. Therefore, the disciples' question—and Jesus' answer—are both very important:

Jesus said unto them, Because of your unbelief.

Matthew 17:20a

Jesus didn't say that it was because they didn't believe or because of their "little faith" (as the *New International Version* and others incorrectly translated it); that's what most people believe. It's possible to believe and yet have unbelief at the same time.

5a. The fact that the disciples didn't ask questions like "Why didn't it work?" implies what?
    That they'd seen 100 percent success
5b. The believers who are the most upset and susceptible to condemnation or feelings that God failed them when they don't see things come to pass are those who know what?
    That faith works
5c. True or false: You can believe and yet have unbelief at the same time.
    True
5d. *Discussion question:* What are some areas in your life in which you have both faith and unbelief?
    Discussion question

DISCIPLESHIP QUESTIONS

1. Only Matthew shows Peter doing what?

    _____

    _____

    _____

2. According to the Gospel of John, what happened when Jesus entered into the ship?

    _____

    _____

    _____

3. Mark recounts some things Jesus said about what?

    _____

    _____

    _____

4. *Discussion question:* What other Bible stories need all four Gospel accounts of them to paint a whole picture?

    _____

    _____

    _____

5. When Peter took his eyes off Jesus and looked at the wind and waves, what did he start to do?

    _____

    _____

    _____

6. Peter had spent his whole life learning that it's better to do what?
    A.   Walk on water
    B.   Fly
    C.   Multitask
    D.   Stay in the boat
    E.   Talk to strangers

7. *Discussion question:* What have you learned to do all of your life that keeps you from stepping out?

    _____

    _____

    _____

8. Jesus said that Peter had _____.
    A.   Weak faith
    B.   Little faith
    C.   No faith
    D.   Strong faith
    E.   A lot of faith

9. True or false: Little faith focused on Jesus is enough to walk on water.

10. The key to the Christian life is_____.
    A.   Little unbelief
    B.   Big faith
    C.   Strong faith
    D.   No faith
    E.   Little belief

11. *Discussion question:* What is the difference between little faith and unbelief?

    _____

    _____

    _____

12. The word *"lunatick"* means that the boy had some type of _____.

13. What was Jesus' reply when he found out the disciples could not cast the demon out?

_____

_____

_____

14. *Discussion question:* What needs can you supernaturally or naturally meet for the people in your life?

_____

_____

_____

15. The fact that the disciples didn't ask questions like "Why didn't it work?" implies what?

_____

_____

_____

16. The believers who are the most upset and susceptible to condemnation or feelings that God failed them when they don't see things come to pass are those who know what?

_____

_____

_____

17. True or false: You can believe and yet have unbelief at the same time.

18. *Discussion question:* What are some areas in your life in which you have both faith and unbelief?

_____

_____

_____

ANSWER KEY

1. Making this request of Jesus and walking on the water

2. The wind ceased, and the ship and all of its occupants were immediately translated to the other shore

3. Hardness of heart

4. *Discussion question*

5. He started focusing on the natural realm

6. D. Stay in the boat

7. *Discussion question*

8. B. Little faith

9. True

10. A. Little unbelief

11. *Discussion question*

12. Seizure

13. *"O faithless and perverse generation"*

14. *Discussion question*

15. That they'd seen 100 percent success

16. That faith works

17. True

18. *Discussion question*

Scriptures

MATTHEW 14:29-33

And he said, Come. And when Peter was come down out of the ship, he walked on the water, to go to Jesus. [30] But when he saw the wind boisterous, he was afraid; and beginning to sink, he cried, saying, Lord, save me. [31] And immediately Jesus stretched forth his hand, and caught him, and said unto him, O thou of little faith, wherefore didst thou doubt? [32] And when they were come into the ship, the wind ceased. [33] Then they that were in the ship came and worshipped him, saying, Of a truth, thou art the Son of God.

JOHN 6:18-21

And the sea arose by reason of a great wind that blew. [19] So when they had rowed about five and twenty or thirty furlongs, they see Jesus walking on the sea, and drawing nigh unto the ship: and they were afraid. [20] But he saith unto them, It is I; be not afraid. [21] Then they willingly received him into the ship: and immediately the ship was at the land whither they went.

HEBREWS 12:2

Looking unto Jesus the author and finisher of our faith; who for the joy that was set before him endured the cross, despising the shame, and is set down at the right hand of the throne of God.

MATTHEW 17:14-20

And when they were come to the multitude, there came to him a certain man, kneeling down to him, and saying, [15] Lord, have mercy on my son: for he is lunatick, and sore vexed: for ofttimes he falleth into the fire, and oft into the water. [16] And I brought him to thy disciples, and they could not cure him. [17] Then Jesus answered and said, O faithless and perverse generation, how long shall I be with you? how long shall I suffer you? bring him hither to me. [18] And Jesus rebuked the devil; and he departed out of him: and the child was cured from that very hour. [19] Then came the disciples to Jesus apart, and said, Why could not we cast him out? [20] Jesus said unto them, Because of your unbelief: for verily I say unto you, If ye have faith as a grain of mustard seed, ye shall say unto this mountain, Remove hence to yonder place; and it shall remove; and nothing shall be impossible unto you.

ONLY BELIEVE

LESSON 12

And they brought him [the demonized boy] *unto him* [Jesus]: *and when he saw him, straightway the spirit tare him; and he fell on the ground, and wallowed foaming. [21] And he asked his father, How long is it ago since this came unto him? And he said, Of a child. [22] And ofttimes it hath cast him into the fire, and into the waters, to destroy him: but if thou canst do any thing, have compassion on us, and help us.*

Mark 9:20-22, brackets mine

This father was beginning to despair. His faith was starting to wane. He said, "**IF** You can do anything." He was beginning to doubt that the deliverance he desired would happen.

Jesus said unto him, If thou canst believe, all things are possible to him that believeth.

Mark 9:23

This man must have had some strong faith to have brought his demonized son to Jesus. If he hadn't been believing for something, he wouldn't have gone to all that effort. Apparently, this boy was so demonized that he was hard to control. He fell on the ground, wallowed, and foamed at the mouth. This father came expecting something, but *"hope deferred maketh the heart sick"* (Prov. 13:12). After seeing the disciples unsuccessfully cast the demon out, the boy falling down and beginning to wallow and foam, and Jesus asking how long he'd been that way, this father was beginning to waver in his faith.

Basically, this man was putting the responsibility back on the Lord when he said, "Jesus, if You can do anything." The Lord turned it right around and put the responsibility back on him, saying, *"If thou canst believe, all things are possible to him that believeth"* (Mark 9:23).

FAITH AND UNBELIEF

Notice the father's response:

And straightway the father of the child cried out, and said with tears, Lord, I believe; help thou mine unbelief.

Mark 9:24

This is significant! The man essentially said, "I have faith, but I also have unbelief. Lord, help me get over my unbelief!" Jesus didn't counter him by answering, "Now, wait a minute. If you have faith, you don't have any unbelief. And if you have any unbelief, you don't have true faith." No, apparently we can have both faith and unbelief at the same time!

The healing of Jairus's daughter reveals the same truth. As the Lord was going to minister to her, He was interrupted by the woman with the issue of blood. He ministered to the woman, and she was completely healed. But—

While he yet spake, there came from the ruler of the synagogue's house certain which said, Thy daughter is dead: why troublest thou the Master any further? [36] As soon as Jesus heard the word that was spoken, he saith unto the ruler of the synagogue, Be not afraid, only believe.

Mark 5:35-36

Why would Jesus tell him to *"only believe"* if believing automatically excludes doubting? Because we can believe and doubt at the same time! That is why the Lord said,

For verily I say unto you, That whosoever shall say unto this mountain, Be thou removed, and be thou cast into the sea; and shall not doubt in his heart, but shall believe that those things which he saith shall come to pass; he shall have whatsoever he saith.

Mark 11:23

Jesus told us to believe, speak in faith, and then doubt not in our hearts. In other words, we can believe and disbelieve at the same time.

PURE FAITH—MINUS UNBELIEF

Now, that's a concept many people don't have. Most Christians don't even take into account the negative effect of unbelief. They just think that the antidote to unbelief is faith. If they recognize the presence of any fear or doubt in their lives, they just try to increase their faith. They attempt to overcome their unbelief with more and more faith. But that's not what the Lord was saying. He basically told the disciples, "If you believe and doubt not" (Mark 11:23). To Jairus, He instructed, *"Only believe"* (Mark 5:36). And the father of the demonized boy said, *"Lord, I believe; help thou mine unbelief"* (Mark 9:24). These are all examples of how faith and unbelief can be present at the same time.

Unbelief is a negative, counterbalancing force that cancels out faith. If a horse was hitched up to a weight, that horse could exert enough strength to move it. But if a horse of equal strength was hitched up and pulling in the opposite direction, the two horses would negate, counteract, and counterbalance each other. The net effect on the weight would be zero.

In Matthew 17, the reason the disciples couldn't cast the demon out wasn't because they didn't have faith. They did have faith. That's why they were asking the question. However, Jesus told them that the problem was their unbelief, which counteracted and negated their faith.

> *And Jesus said unto them, Because of your unbelief: for verily I say unto you, If ye have faith as a grain of mustard seed, ye shall say unto this mountain, Remove hence to yonder place; and it shall remove; and nothing shall be impossible unto you.*
>
> Matthew 17:20

Jesus declared, "It's because of your unbelief!" Then He continued, saying, "If you have faith like a grain of mustard seed." Since a mustard seed is very tiny, the Lord was basically saying, "You don't need huge faith. If your faith is as big as a mustard seed, it's enough to see a mountain cast into the sea. You just need a pure faith minus unbelief!"

CONFUSED

Most Christians have the false concept that unbelief is something they can't really deal with. It's just there, and all they have to do is increase their faith level to overcome it.

Imagine two thermometers. One is a faith-o-meter and the other is an unbelief-o-meter. We need to constantly monitor both meters. Most people don't even acknowledge, quantify, or gauge the amount of unbelief in their lives. They just think that having fear, worry, or stress or being hurt and falling apart when the doctor tells them they are going to die is just normal. They don't even think about this or do anything to deal with their unbelief. They just try to increase their measure of faith. So, they read the Word more, pray more, and do other things in an effort to increase and build more and more faith.

This is contrary to everything Jesus taught. He essentially said, "If you have faith as a grain of mustard seed, it's enough to cast a mountain into the sea. You don't need a huge faith. You just need a faith that isn't diluted, counterbalanced, and negated by unbelief."

I'm sure you've probably seen faith work. You've seen God answer your prayers, heal you, deliver you, or do something for you or someone you've prayed for. But then you prayed for someone else, expecting the same result, but didn't see it. It's really confusing, because you know you have faith. But do you have unbelief?

Not long after I'd seen my first person raised from the dead, I remember being so excited! I not only believed in theory that God could do miracles, but I also saw it happen. And I was pumped! While holding a meeting in Omaha, Nebraska, I noticed a man in a wheelchair to my left in the front row. I could hardly wait to get through preaching so that I could go over there and see him come out of that wheelchair. I reasoned, *If you could see a man raised from the dead, then surely you could see someone come out of a wheelchair.* So, I went over and grabbed him by the hand and declared, "In the name of Jesus, rise up and walk!" I yanked him up out of that chair, and he fell right over on his face. Since he was paralyzed, he couldn't even brace himself to break the fall.

When that happened, people gasped. You could hear their groans. I groaned too. You could actually hear the unbelief. It was tangible, and I didn't know what to do. So, I bent down on my knees, took hold of the man, hugged him, wrestled him back into his wheelchair, and said the scriptural equivalent of *"Depart in peace, be ye warmed and filled"* (James 2:16). But I didn't give him what he needed.

I returned to my hotel room that night, confused, saying, "God, I don't understand." What made it so bad was that I had truly expected that man to be healed. I knew I had faith for him to be made whole. You don't just pull a paralyzed guy up out of a wheelchair in front of lots of other people unless you fully expect him to get up and walk. If I'd ever thought about him falling flat on his face, I wouldn't have done that. I knew I had faith. That's what confused and hurt me so much. If I hadn't had faith but had been in fear and thinking *O God, I know this isn't going to work, but I'll do it anyway*, I wouldn't have been surprised. However, I was surprised because I wholeheartedly expected him to be able to walk. I just couldn't understand why this happened. It took me approximately three years to learn some things before I understood why.

ANDREW'S RECOMMENDATIONS FOR FURTHER STUDY

Most of what the Lord taught me about the situation with the man in the wheelchair is included in my *Hardness of Heart* teaching.

OUTLINE

I.   The father in Mark 9:20-23 was beginning to despair and doubt that the deliverance he desired would happen.

> *And they brought him* [the demonized boy] *unto him* [Jesus]: *and when he saw him, straightway the spirit tare him; and he fell on the ground, and wallowed foaming.* [21] *And he asked his father, How long is it ago since this came unto him? And he said, Of a child.* [22] *And ofttimes it hath cast him into the fire, and into the waters, to destroy him: but if thou canst do any thing, have compassion on us, and help us.* [23] *Jesus said unto him, If thou canst believe, all things are possible to him that believeth.*
>
> Mark 9:20-23, brackets mine

A.   This man must have had some strong faith to have brought his demonized son to Jesus—if he hadn't been believing for something, he wouldn't have gone to all that effort.

B.   This father came expecting something, but *"hope deferred maketh the heart sick"* (Prov. 13:12); he was beginning to waver in his faith.

C.   Basically, this man was putting the responsibility back on the Lord when he said, "Jesus, if You can do anything."

D.   The Lord turned it right around and put the responsibility back on him, saying, *"If thou canst believe, all things are possible to him that believeth"* (Mark 9:23).

II. We need to notice the father's response—it's significant:

> *And straightway the father of the child cried out, and said with tears, Lord, I believe; help thou mine unbelief.*
>
> Mark 9:24

A.   Apparently we can have both faith and unbelief at the same time!

B.   The healing of Jairus's daughter reveals the same truth.

> *While he yet spake, there came from the ruler of the synagogue's house certain which said, Thy daughter is dead: why troublest thou the Master*

any further? [36] As soon as Jesus heard the word that was spoken, he saith unto the ruler of the synagogue, Be not afraid, only believe.

Mark 5:35-36

C. Why would Jesus tell him to *"only believe"* if believing automatically excludes doubting?

D. Because we can believe and doubt at the same time!

For verily I say unto you, That whosoever shall say unto this mountain, Be thou removed, and be thou cast into the sea; and shall not doubt in his heart, but shall believe that those things which he saith shall come to pass; he shall have whatsoever he saith.

Mark 11:23

E. Jesus told us to believe, speak in faith, and then doubt not in our hearts.

III. Most Christians don't even take into account the negative effect of unbelief.

A. They just think that the antidote to unbelief is faith, but that's not what the Lord was saying.

B. Unbelief is a negative, counterbalancing force that cancels out faith.

C. In Matthew 17, the reason the disciples couldn't cast the demon out wasn't because they didn't have faith—Jesus told them that the problem was their unbelief, which counteracted and negated their faith:

And Jesus said unto them, Because of your unbelief: for verily I say unto you, If ye have faith as a grain of mustard seed, ye shall say unto this mountain, Remove hence to yonder place; and it shall remove; and nothing shall be impossible unto you.

Matthew 17:20

D. You just need a pure faith minus unbelief!

IV. Most Christians have the false concept that unbelief is something they can't really deal with.

A. It's just there, and all they have to do is increase their faith level to overcome it.

B. This is contrary to everything Jesus taught.

C. You've probably seen faith work, but then you prayed for someone else, expecting the same result, but didn't see it.

D. It's really confusing, because you know you have faith—but do you have unbelief?

ANDREW'S RECOMMENDATIONS FOR FURTHER STUDY

Most of what the Lord taught Andrew about the situation with the man in the wheelchair is included in his *Hardness of Heart* teaching.

TEACHER'S GUIDE

1. The father in Mark 9:20-23 was beginning to despair and doubt that the deliverance he desired would happen.

> *And they brought him* [the demonized boy] *unto him* [Jesus]: *and when he saw him, straightway the spirit tare him; and he fell on the ground, and wallowed foaming.* [21] *And he asked his father, How long is it ago since this came unto him? And he said, Of a child.* [22] *And ofttimes it hath cast him into the fire, and into the waters, to destroy him: but if thou canst do any thing, have compassion on us, and help us.* [23] *Jesus said unto him, If thou canst believe, all things are possible to him that believeth.*
>
> Mark 9:20-23, brackets mine

This man must have had some strong faith to have brought his demonized son to Jesus—if he hadn't been believing for something, he wouldn't have gone to all that effort. This father came expecting something, but *"hope deferred maketh the heart sick"* (Prov. 13:12); he was beginning to waver in his faith. Basically, this man was putting the responsibility back on the Lord when he said, "Jesus, if You can do anything." The Lord turned it right around and put the responsibility back on him, saying, *"If thou canst believe, all things are possible to him that believeth"* (Mark 9:23).

1a. Even though the father in Mark 9 was beginning to doubt that his son would be delivered, how did he show that he had strong faith?
    He brought his son to Jesus
1b. *Discussion question*: The father came to Jesus for help, so why did Jesus put the responsibility back on him (Mark 9:23)?
    Discussion question

2. We need to notice the father's response—it's significant:

> *And straightway the father of the child cried out, and said with tears, Lord, I believe; help thou mine unbelief.*
>
> Mark 9:24

Apparently we can have both faith and unbelief at the same time! The healing of Jairus's daughter reveals the same truth.

> *While he yet spake, there came from the ruler of the synagogue's house certain which said, Thy daughter is dead: why troublest thou the Master*

any further? [36] As soon as Jesus heard the word that was spoken, he saith unto the ruler of the synagogue, Be not afraid, only believe.

Mark 5:35-36

Why would Jesus tell him to *"only believe"* if believing automatically excludes doubting? Because we can believe and doubt at the same time!

> *For verily I say unto you, That whosoever shall say unto this mountain, Be thou removed, and be thou cast into the sea; and shall not doubt in his heart, but shall believe that those things which he saith shall come to pass; he shall have whatsoever he saith.*

Mark 11:23

Jesus told us to believe, speak in faith, and then doubt not in our hearts.

2a. *Discussion question:* What can you learn from the father's response to Jesus (Mark 9:24)?
   Discussion question

2b. What same truth does the healing of Jairus's daughter reveal?
   You can have both faith and unbelief at the same time

2c. Jesus said to _____, _____ in faith, and then _____ not in your heart.
   Believe / speak / doubt

2d. *Discussion question:* In light of what Jesus said in Mark 11:23, discuss how receiving from God is a combination of believing, speaking, and not doubting.
   Discussion question

3. Most Christians don't even take into account the negative effect of unbelief. They just think that the antidote to unbelief is faith, but that's not what the Lord was saying. Unbelief is a negative, counterbalancing force that cancels out faith. In Matthew 17, the reason the disciples couldn't cast the demon out wasn't because they didn't have faith—Jesus told them that the problem was their unbelief, which counteracted and negated their faith:

> *And Jesus said unto them, Because of your unbelief: for verily I say unto you, If ye have faith as a grain of mustard seed, ye shall say unto this mountain, Remove hence to yonder place; and it shall remove; and nothing shall be impossible unto you.*

Matthew 17:20

We just need a pure faith minus unbelief!

3a. What do most Christians not even take into account?
  A. The stock market
  B. The negative effect of little faith
  C. The negative effect of unbelief
  D. All of the above
  E. None of the above
  C. The negative effect of unbelief
3b. True or false: Faith is the antidote to unbelief.
  False
3c. What does unbelief do to your faith?
  It cancels it out
3d. *Discussion question:* What does "pure faith with little unbelief" look like in everyday life?
  Discussion question

4. Most Christians have the false concept that unbelief is something they can't really deal with. It's just there, and all they have to do is increase their faith level to overcome it. This is contrary to everything Jesus taught. We've probably seen faith work, but then we prayed for someone else, expecting the same result, but didn't see it. It's really confusing, because we know we have faith—but do we have unbelief?

4a. True or false: Unbelief is something you can't really deal with.
  False
4b. Trying to increase your faith is _____ to everything Jesus taught.
  Contrary
4c. *Discussion question:* What are some areas in your life where you are experiencing confusion because you have faith but you may also have unbelief?
  Discussion question

DISCIPLESHIP QUESTIONS

1. Even though the father in Mark 9 was beginning to doubt that his son would be delivered, how did he show that he had strong faith?

   _____

   _____

   _____

2. *Discussion question:* The father came to Jesus for help, so why did Jesus put the responsibility back on him (Mark 9:23)?

   _____

   _____

   _____

3. *Discussion question:* What can you learn from the father's response to Jesus (Mark 9:24)?

   _____

   _____

   _____

4. What same truth does the healing of Jairus's daughter reveal?

   _____

   _____

   _____

5. Jesus said to _____, _____ in faith, and then _____ not in your heart.

6. *Discussion question:* In light of what Jesus said in Mark 11:23, discuss how receiving from God is a combination of believing, speaking, and not doubting.

_____

_____

_____

7. What do most Christians not even take into account?
   A. The stock market
   B. The negative effect of little faith
   C. The negative effect of unbelief
   D. All of the above
   E. None of the above

8. True or false: Faith is the antidote to unbelief.

9. What does unbelief do to your faith?

_____

_____

_____

10. *Discussion question:* What does "pure faith with little unbelief" look like in everyday life?

_____

_____

_____

11. True or false: Unbelief is something you can't really deal with.

12. Trying to increase your faith is _____ to everything Jesus taught.

13. *Discussion question:* What are some areas in your life where you are experiencing confusion because you have faith but you may also have unbelief?

_____

_____

_____

ANSWER KEY

1. He brought his son to Jesus

2. *Discussion question*

3. *Discussion question*

4. You can have both faith and unbelief at the same time

5. Believe / speak / doubt

6. *Discussion question*

7. C. The negative effect of unbelief

8. False

9. It cancels it out

10. *Discussion question*

11. False

12. Contrary

13. *Discussion question*

Scriptures

MARK 9:20-24

And they brought him unto him: and when he saw him, straightway the spirit tare him; and he fell on the ground, and wallowed foaming. [21] And he asked his father, How long is it ago since this came unto him? And he said, Of a child. [22] And ofttimes it hath cast him into the fire, and into the waters, to destroy him: but if thou canst do any thing, have compassion on us, and help us. [23] Jesus said unto him, If thou canst believe, all things are possible to him that believeth. [24] And straightway the father of the child cried out, and said with tears, Lord, I believe; help thou mine unbelief.

PROVERBS 13:12

Hope deferred maketh the heart sick: but when the desire cometh, it is a tree of life.

MARK 5:35-36

While he yet spake, there came from the ruler of the synagogue's house certain which said, Thy daughter is dead: why troublest thou the Master any further? [36] As soon as Jesus heard the word that was spoken, he saith unto the ruler of the synagogue, Be not afraid, only believe.

MARK 11:23

For verily I say unto you, That whosoever shall say unto this mountain, Be thou removed, and be thou cast into the sea; and shall not doubt in his heart, but shall believe that those things which he saith shall come to pass; he shall have whatsoever he saith.

MATTHEW 17:20

And Jesus said unto them, Because of your unbelief: for verily I say unto you, If ye have faith as a grain of mustard seed, ye shall say unto this mountain, Remove hence to yonder place; and it shall remove; and nothing shall be impossible unto you.

JAMES 2:16

And one of you say unto them, Depart in peace, be ye warmed and filled; notwithstanding ye give them not those things which are needful to the body; what doth it profit?

UNBELIEF WILL SINK YOU

LESSON 13

While reading a book about Smith Wigglesworth, I discovered that he used to start his miracle services by boldly declaring, "The first person to come up here on the stage will be healed of whatever you have!" Someone would come up, and he would pray for them, see them healed, and then preach about how it happened. Then he would give an altar call, go through and lay hands on people, and see many, many folks healed. Wigglesworth saw lots of great miracles this way.

At one of Wigglesworth's meetings, two ladies brought an elderly friend who was suffering from a cancerous tumor. As soon as he said, "The first person up here gets healed," they rushed their friend up to the stage. The tumor on this woman was so large that it made her look like she was nine months' pregnant. She was so weak that she couldn't stand without her two friends' assistance. They stood on the stage, one on each side of her, holding her up. Smith looked at them and said, "Let her go."

They answered, "We can't let her go. She'll fall."

Wigglesworth raised his voice a little and told them, "I said let her go." They did, and she fell forward, on top of that tumor, groaning out loud in pain. The people in the crowd began to gasp and moan—exactly like they did when I pulled that man out of the wheelchair and he fell on his face (mentioned in the last lesson).

Smith Wigglesworth didn't have any more faith when he ministered to that woman than I did when I ministered to that man (Rom. 12:3). The difference was that Wigglesworth had less unbelief. When I prayed for the man in the wheelchair and he fell flat on his face, I responded in confusion, shame, guilt, and fear. I grabbed him and helped him back up into his wheelchair. Smith just kept right on going and said, "Pick her up."

They picked the woman up and stood her in front of Wigglesworth again. He said, "Let her go."

The two women responded, "We can't let her go. She'll fall again!"

Wigglesworth yelled at them, "I said let her go!" They did, and she fell flat on that tumor again. He said, "Pick her up." They did. Then he told them, "Let her go."

They answered, "We will not let her go!"

Smith barked, "I said let her go!"

At that point, a man in the audience stood up and declared, "You beast! Leave that poor woman alone!"

Smith got mad and hollered, "I know my business. You mind your own!" Then he turned to the women and ordered, "You let her go!" They did, and that tumor fell out of her dress onto the stage, and the woman walked off totally healed.

Wigglesworth didn't have any more faith than I did; he just had less unbelief. Can you see the difference?

TRUSTING IN GOD

When Jesus' disciples asked "Why couldn't we cast the demon out?" Jesus answered, "Because of your unbelief!" The reason they asked this question in the first place was because they truly believed and were expecting. They'd seen their faith work on other people, but they didn't see the desired results this time. The Lord basically told them, "Guys, it's not because you didn't have faith. If your faith is only the size of a mustard seed, it's sufficient. You don't need huge faith. Just deal with your unbelief!" This is what most Christians are not doing. They aren't dealing with their unbelief.

Faith is simply trusting in God. It is having thoughts, feelings, and emotions that are consistent with the Word of God. The Lord said that we would lay hands on the sick and they would recover (Mark 16:18). If we say "I can do that; I'm going to do that" and start seeing it on the inside, getting excited about it, and then acting on it, that's faith.

Unbelief is the opposite. Unbelief is thoughts, feelings, emotions, and actions that are opposed to what God's Word says. Most Christians aren't doing anything to deal with the negative force of unbelief. They're just trying to increase their faith.

People often come to one of my meetings, hear me talking faith, see miracles, and go right home and try to do the same thing. Then they get frustrated and disappointed when they don't get the same results. When I talk to them, they tell me that they go to a church that doesn't even believe in the baptism of the Holy Spirit and speaking in tongues. Instead of preaching on faith, their church emphasizes the false doctrine commonly called "the sovereignty of God," which says that maybe God makes people sick to teach them a lesson. They're around all this unbelief but don't even take that into account. They think they can just go back, speak the Word, and everything will work. Even Jesus—who always operated in faith perfectly—couldn't do many mighty works in His hometown due to the people's unbelief. The atmosphere of unbelief in a given area or group of people can affect even someone who is operating in faith perfectly.

> *And he could there do no mighty work, save that he laid his hands upon a few sick folk, and healed them. [6] And he marvelled because of their unbelief.*
>
> Mark 6:5-6

It's not just a matter of the power we exert; it's also a matter of all the negative things around us. That's why when Jesus raised Jairus's daughter from the dead, He only allowed the father, mother, and a couple of disciples to be there. He put out all the people who were mocking, scorning, and laughing at Him.

> *And, behold, there cometh one of the rulers of the synagogue, Jairus by name; and when he saw him, he fell at his feet, [23] And besought him greatly, saying, My little daughter lieth at the point of death: I pray thee, come and lay thy hands on her, that she may be healed; and she shall live. [24] And Jesus went with him; and much people followed him, and thronged him.*
>
> Mark 5:22-24

> *While he yet spake, there came from the ruler of the synagogue's house certain which said, Thy daughter is dead: why troublest thou the Master any further? [36] As soon as Jesus heard the word that was spoken, he saith unto the ruler of the synagogue, Be not afraid, only believe. [37] And he suffered no man to follow him, save Peter, and James, and John the brother of James. [38] And he cometh to the house of the ruler of the synagogue, and seeth the tumult, and them that wept and wailed greatly. [39] And when he was come in, he saith unto them, Why make ye this ado, and weep? the damsel is not dead, but sleepeth. [40] And they laughed him to scorn. But when he had put them all out, he taketh the father and the mother of the damsel, and them that were with him, and entereth in where the damsel was lying. [41] And he took the damsel by the hand, and said unto her, Talitha cumi; which is, being interpreted, Damsel, I say unto thee, arise. [42] And straightway the damsel arose, and walked; for she was of the age of twelve years. And they were astonished with a great astonishment. [43] And he charged them straitly*

*that no man should know it; and commanded that something should be
given her to eat.*

Mark 5:35-43

When Elijah, Elisha, and Peter raised people from the dead, they all sought
seclusion (1 Kin. 17:17-24, 2 Kin. 4:32-37, and Acts 9:36-41). They separated from
the unbelievers and got rid of unbelief. It's the same principle. They had faith, but they
didn't want any unbelief around to counter their faith.

DEAL WITH UNBELIEF

I meet people constantly who don't even consider the unbelief of others. They just
want to go marching in to a hospital and see someone raised up. They don't take into
account that not everybody there believes in these things but, instead, is resistant and
critical toward them. Therefore, we must take into account the unbelief of other people.

Bethsaida was one of the most unbelieving, resistant places to the Lord's ministry
of anywhere He'd been.

*Woe unto thee, Bethsaida! for if the mighty works had been done in
Tyre and Sidon, which have been done in you, they had a great while ago
repented, sitting in sackcloth and ashes.*

Luke 10:13

When Jesus encountered a man there who was blind, He had to take him by the
hand and lead him away from all of the unbelief. Even when He had gotten the man
out of the town, He knew He hadn't gotten "all of the town" out of the man. Jesus
had to pray for him twice. This is the only time in Scripture that Jesus prayed twice
for someone. Finally, once the man saw clearly, Jesus told him not to go back into that
town or tell anyone there about his healing, because of their unbelief (Mark 8:22-26).

Very few people are doing much to deal with unbelief. They just try to be strong in
faith. However, we need to recognize that just as faith comes by hearing the Word of
God, unbelief comes by hearing things contrary to the Word of God. If we are going
to be really strong and see our faith produce, we need to cut off the inroad of unbelief
into our lives. We simply cannot allow the sewage of this world to flow through our
minds and emotions without it affecting our unbelief levels. Unbelief comes through
hearing things opposed to God's Word just like faith comes by hearing things that are
in agreement with God's Word.

LOOKING UNTO HIM

As long as Peter looked to Jesus, the Author and Finisher of our faith (Heb. 12:2), he walked on water. But when he took his eyes off the Lord, he began to see the wind and the waves. Although the wind and the waves weren't demonic or evil, they were contrary to faith.

At times, a breeze can be a wonderful thing. It can cool us off and be very pleasant. Waves aren't bad either. It's actually very soothing to sit on the shore and see waves. However, it's different when they're extreme. The howling wind and tall waves overwhelmed Peter with unbelief. He probably started thinking thoughts like, *I shouldn't be out on this water. I need to get back into the boat!* Most likely, if he started having these thoughts, that's when he began to sink.

Notice how Peter didn't just plop down all at once and instantly sink. The Word says that he *began* to sink (Matt. 14:30). Likewise, unbelief doesn't come all at once. It doesn't just jump on us like a seizure. Like faith, unbelief comes gradually through the way we think. We must build and grow ourselves in this area. Peter didn't just lose his faith and start operating in unbelief all at once. It was something that happened gradually.

Peter had enough sense to turn to Jesus and call out for help. He could have called back to the guys in the boat. He could have just totally given up all faith and thought, *This is crazy. This must not be Jesus. This must be a vision. What am I doing out here?* Peter could have yelled for the guys in the boat to throw him a rope, but instead, he turned back to Jesus.

There is no indication that Jesus carried Peter back to the boat. The Word implies that they walked back together. Peter walked on the water again but, this time, hand in hand with Jesus and looking unto Him.

WHAT ARE YOU THINKING?

Lack of faith didn't cause Peter to sink—unbelief did. He began to sink when he took his eyes off Jesus. The reason most Christians never walk on water is because they aren't really looking at Jesus the way they should. If they start walking in a miracle but struggle and begin to sink, it's because they have taken their eyes off Jesus. They are considering what the banker, doctor, family member, or checkbook is saying instead of what God's Word says. They have started thinking about something else. It's not that they don't have faith; it's just that their faith is being negated and counterbalanced by their unbelief that is pulling in the opposite direction.

Outline

I. When Jesus' disciples asked "Why couldn't we cast the demon out?" Jesus answered, "Because of your unbelief!"

    A. Faith is simply trusting in God; it is having thoughts, feelings, and emotions that are consistent with the Word of God.

    B. Unbelief is thoughts, feelings, emotions, and actions that are opposed to what God's Word says.

    C. The atmosphere of unbelief in a given area or group of people can affect even someone who is operating in faith perfectly, like Jesus—

       And he could there do no mighty work, save that he laid his hands upon a few sick folk, and healed them. [6] And he marvelled because of their unbelief.

                                            Mark 6:5-6

    D. It's not just a matter of the power we exert; it's also a matter of all the negative things around us.

    E. When Elijah, Elisha, and Peter raised people from the dead, they all sought seclusion (1 Kin. 17:17-24, 2 Kin. 4:32-37, and Acts 9:36-41).

    F. They had faith, but they didn't want any unbelief around to counter their faith.

II. We must take into account the unbelief of other people.

    A. When Jesus encountered a man in Bethsaida who was blind, He had to lead him away from all of the unbelief (Luke 10:13 and Mark 8:22-26).

       i. Even when He had gotten the man out of the town, He knew He hadn't gotten "all of the town" out of the man and had to pray for him twice.

    B. If we are going to be really strong and see our faith produce, we need to cut off the inroad of unbelief into our lives.

    C. Unbelief comes through hearing things opposed to God's Word just like faith comes by hearing things that are in agreement with God's Word.

III. As long as Peter looked to Jesus, he walked on water, but when he took his eyes off the Lord, the howling wind and tall waves overwhelmed him with unbelief.

A. Peter didn't instantly sink; the Word says that he *began* to sink (Matt. 14:30).

B. Likewise, unbelief doesn't come all at once—it comes gradually through the way we think.

C. Peter had enough sense to turn to Jesus and call out for help.

   i. He could have called back to the guys in the boat and totally given up all faith.

D. The Word implies that they walked back together; Peter walked on the water again, but with Jesus, looking unto Him.

IV. Lack of faith didn't cause Peter to sink—unbelief did.

A. The reason most Christians never walk on water is because they aren't really looking at Jesus the way they should.

B. If they start walking in a miracle but struggle and begin to sink, it's because they have taken their eyes off Jesus.

C. It's not that they don't have faith; it's just that their faith is being negated and counterbalanced by their unbelief that is pulling in the opposite direction.

TEACHER'S GUIDE

1. When Jesus' disciples asked "Why couldn't we cast the demon out?" Jesus answered, "Because of your unbelief!" Faith is simply trusting in God; it is having thoughts, feelings, and emotions that are consistent with the Word of God. Unbelief is thoughts, feelings, emotions, and actions that are opposed to what God's Word says. The atmosphere of unbelief in a given area or group of people can affect even someone who is operating in faith perfectly, like Jesus—

> And he could there do no mighty work, save that he laid his hands upon a few sick folk, and healed them. [6] And he marvelled because of their unbelief.
>
> Mark 6:5-6

It's not just a matter of the power we exert; it's also a matter of all the negative things around us. When Elijah, Elisha, and Peter raised people from the dead, they all sought seclusion (1 Kin. 17:17-24, 2 Kin. 4:32-37, and Acts 9:36-41). They had faith, but they didn't want any unbelief around to counter their faith.

1a. Faith is simply _____ in God.
 Trusting
1b. What is unbelief?
 Thoughts, feelings, emotions, and actions that are opposed to God's Word
1c. *Discussion question:* What are some ways that you can deal with your unbelief?
 Discussion question
1d. True or false: An atmosphere of unbelief can affect someone who is operating in faith.
 True
1e. *Discussion question:* Why is the spiritual atmosphere an important part of walking in miracles?
 Discussion question

2. We must take into account the unbelief of other people. When Jesus encountered a man in Bethsaida who was blind, He had to lead him away from all of the unbelief (Luke 10:13 and Mark 8:22-26). Even when He had gotten the man out of the town, He knew He hadn't gotten "all of the town" out of the man and had to pray for him twice. If we are going to be really strong and see our faith produce, we need to cut off the inroad of unbelief into our lives. Unbelief comes through hearing things opposed to God's Word just like faith comes by hearing things that are in agreement with God's Word.

2a. People don't consider the unbelief of _____.
   A. Their dog
   B. Their ancestors
   C. Others
   D. All of the above
   E. None of the above
   C. Others
2b. How does unbelief come?
   Through hearing things opposed to God's Word
2c. *Discussion question*: Why do you think faith and unbelief are strengthened by what you hear?
   Discussion question

3. As long as Peter looked to Jesus, he walked on water, but when he took his eyes off the Lord, the howling wind and tall waves overwhelmed Peter with unbelief. Peter didn't instantly sink; the Word says that he *began* to sink (Matt. 14:30). Likewise, unbelief doesn't come all at once—it comes gradually through the way we think. Peter had enough sense to turn to Jesus and call out for help. He could have called back to the guys in the boat and totally given up all faith. The Word implies that they walked back together; Peter walked on the water again, but with Jesus, looking unto Him.

3a. True or false: Peter instantly sank when he took his eyes off the Lord.
   False
3b. Unbelief comes _____ through the way you think.
   Gradually
3c. *Discussion question*: What are some thought processes of unbelief?
   Discussion question
3d. *Discussion question*: Where do you look for help—instead of looking to Jesus?
   Discussion question

4. Lack of faith didn't cause Peter to sink—unbelief did. The reason most Christians never walk on water is because they aren't really looking at Jesus the way they should. If they start walking in a miracle but struggle and begin to sink, it's because they have taken their eyes off Jesus. It's not that they don't have faith; it's just that their faith is being negated and counterbalanced by their unbelief that is pulling in the opposite direction.

4a. True or false: Lack of faith caused Peter to sink.
False

4b. Why do most Christians never walk on water?
They aren't looking at Jesus the way they should

4c. *Discussion question:* How does unbelief negate and counterbalance faith?
Discussion question

DISCIPLESHIP QUESTIONS

1.   Faith is simply _____ in God.

2.   What is unbelief?

     _____

     _____

     _____

3.   *Discussion question:* What are some ways that you can deal with your unbelief?

     _____

     _____

     _____

4.   True or false: An atmosphere of unbelief can affect someone who is operating in faith.

5.   *Discussion question:* Why is the spiritual atmosphere an important part of walking in miracles?

     _____

     _____

     _____

6.   People don't consider the unbelief of _____.
     A.   Their dog
     B.   Their ancestors
     C.   Others
     D.   All of the above
     E.   None of the above

7.   How does unbelief come?

_____

_____

_____

8.   *Discussion question:* Why do you think faith and unbelief are strengthened by
     what you hear?

_____

_____

_____

9.   True or false: Peter instantly sank when he took his eyes off the Lord.

10. Unbelief comes _____ through the way you think.

11. *Discussion question:* What are some thought processes of unbelief?

_____

_____

_____

12. *Discussion question:* Where do you look for help—instead of looking to Jesus?

_____

_____

_____

13. True or false: Lack of faith caused Peter to sink.

14. Why do most Christians never walk on water?

    _____

    _____

    _____

15. *Discussion question:* How does unbelief negate and counterbalance faith?

    _____

    _____

    _____

ANSWER KEY

1. Trusting

2. Thoughts, feelings, emotions, and actions that are opposed to God's Word

3. *Discussion question*

4. True

5. *Discussion question*

6. C. Others

7. Through hearing things opposed to God's Word

8. *Discussion question*

9. False

10. Gradually

11. *Discussion question*

12. *Discussion question*

13. False

14. They aren't looking at Jesus the way they should

15. *Discussion question*

SCRIPTURES

ROMANS 12:3

For I say, through the grace given unto me, to every man that is among you, not to think of himself more highly than he ought to think; but to think soberly, according as God hath dealt to every man the measure of faith.

MARK 16:18

They shall take up serpents; and if they drink any deadly thing, it shall not hurt them; they shall lay hands on the sick, and they shall recover.

MARK 6:5-6

And he could there do no mighty work, save that he laid his hands upon a few sick folk, and healed them. [6] And he marvelled because of their unbelief. And he went round about the villages, teaching.

MARK 5:22-24

And, behold, there cometh one of the rulers of the synagogue, Jairus by name; and when he saw him, he fell at his feet, [23] And besought him greatly, saying, My little daughter lieth at the point of death: I pray thee, come and lay thy hands on her, that she may be healed; and she shall live. [24] And Jesus went with him; and much people followed him, and thronged him.

MARK 5:35-43

While he yet spake, there came from the ruler of the synagogue's house certain which said, Thy daughter is dead: why troublest thou the Master any further? [36] As soon as Jesus heard the word that was spoken, he saith unto the ruler of the synagogue, Be not afraid, only believe. [37] And he suffered no man to follow him, save Peter, and James, and John the brother of James. [38] And he cometh to the house of the ruler of the synagogue, and seeth the tumult, and them that wept and wailed greatly. [39] And when he was come in, he saith unto them, Why make ye this ado, and weep? the damsel is not dead, but sleepeth. [40] And they laughed him to scorn. But when he had put them all out, he taketh the father and the mother of the damsel, and them that were with him, and entereth in where the damsel was lying. [41] And he took the damsel by the hand, and said unto her, Talitha cumi; which is, being interpreted,

Damsel, I say unto thee, arise. [42] And straightway the damsel arose, and walked; for she was of the age of twelve years. And they were astonished with a great astonishment. [43] And he charged them straitly that no man should know it; and commanded that something should be given her to eat.

1 KINGS 17:17-24

And it came to pass after these things, that the son of the woman, the mistress of the house, fell sick; and his sickness was so sore, that there was no breath left in him. [18] And she said unto Elijah, What have I to do with thee, O thou man of God? art thou come unto me to call my sin to remembrance, and to slay my son? [19] And he said unto her, Give me thy son. And he took him out of her bosom, and carried him up into a loft, where he abode, and laid him upon his own bed. [20] And he cried unto the LORD, and said, O LORD my God, hast thou also brought evil upon the widow with whom I sojourn, by slaying her son? [21] And he stretched himself upon the child three times, and cried unto the LORD, and said, O LORD my God, I pray thee, let this child's soul come into him again. [22] And the LORD heard the voice of Elijah; and the soul of the child came into him again, and he revived. [23] And Elijah took the child, and brought him down out of the chamber into the house, and delivered him unto his mother: and Elijah said, See, thy son liveth. [24] And the woman said to Elijah, Now by this I know that thou art a man of God, and that the word of the LORD in thy mouth is truth.

2 KINGS 4:32-37

And when Elisha was come into the house, behold, the child was dead, and laid upon his bed. [33] He went in therefore, and shut the door upon them twain, and prayed unto the LORD. [34] And he went up, and lay upon the child, and put his mouth upon his mouth, and his eyes upon his eyes, and his hands upon his hands: and he stretched himself upon the child; and the flesh of the child waxed warm. [35] Then he returned, and walked in the house to and fro; and went up, and stretched himself upon him: and the child sneezed seven times, and the child opened his eyes. [36] And he called Gehazi, and said, Call this Shunammite. So he called her. And when she was come in unto him, he said, Take up thy son. [37] Then she went in, and fell at his feet, and bowed herself to the ground, and took up her son, and went out.

ACTS 9:36-41

Now there was at Joppa a certain disciple named Tabitha, which by interpretation is called Dorcas: this woman was full of good works and almsdeeds which she did. [37] And it came to pass in those days, that she was sick, and died: whom when they had washed, they laid her in an upper chamber. [38] And forasmuch as Lydda was nigh to Joppa, and the disciples had heard that Peter was there, they sent unto him two men, desiring him that he would not delay to come to them. [39] Then Peter arose and went with them. When he was come, they brought him into the upper chamber: and all the widows stood by him weeping, and shewing the coats and garments which Dorcas made, while she was with them. [40] But Peter put them all forth, and kneeled down, and prayed; and turning him to the body said, Tabitha, arise. And she opened her eyes: and when she saw Peter, she sat up. [41] And he gave her his hand, and lifted her up, and when he had called the saints and widows, presented her alive.

LUKE 10:13

Woe unto thee, Chorazin! woe unto thee, Bethsaida! for if the mighty works had been done in Tyre and Sidon, which have been done in you, they had a great while ago repented, sitting in sackcloth and ashes.

MARK 8:22-26

And he cometh to Bethsaida; and they bring a blind man unto him, and besought him to touch him. [23] And he took the blind man by the hand, and led him out of the town; and when he had spit on his eyes, and put his hands upon him, he asked him if he saw ought. [24] And he looked up, and said, I see men as trees, walking. [25] After that he put his hands again upon his eyes, and made him look up: and he was restored, and saw every man clearly. [26] And he sent him away to his house, saying, Neither go into the town, nor tell it to any in the town.

HEBREWS 12:2

Looking unto Jesus the author and finisher of our faith; who for the joy that was set before him endured the cross, despising the shame, and is set down at the right hand of the throne of God.

MATTHEW 14:30

But when he saw the wind boisterous, he was afraid; and beginning to sink, he cried, saying, Lord, save me.

A Pure Faith

LESSON 14

Miracles don't require huge faith—just a pure and simple faith. When the disciples asked Jesus to increase their faith, He responded in Luke 17 very much the same as he did in Mark 11.

> *And the apostles said unto the Lord, Increase our faith. [6] And the Lord said, If ye had faith as a grain of mustard seed, ye might say unto this sycamine tree, Be thou plucked up by the root, and be thou planted in the sea; and it should obey you.*
>
> Luke 17:5-6

In other words, Jesus was saying, "Guys, you don't need more faith. Your faith is sufficient. If your faith is only the size of a mustard seed, it's enough to uproot a tree without touching it. Just by speaking to it, you can make it leave." Then He continued, using the example of a slave:

> *But which of you, having a servant plowing or feeding cattle, will say unto him by and by, when he is come from the field, Go and sit down to meat? [8] And will not rather say unto him, Make ready wherewith I may sup, and gird thyself, and serve me, till I have eaten and drunken; and afterward thou shalt eat and drink?*
>
> Luke 17:7-8

Jesus was basically saying, "When you have a slave, you use them. The problem isn't that you don't have enough faith. It's the fact that you aren't using what you already have!" If you could understand this, it would answer some of the questions you've had, questions like, "I know I believed, so why didn't it work?" It's not because you weren't believing; it's because you were believing and disbelieving at the same time!

The way you overcome your problem isn't by trying to get huge faith. If you believe that God heals, that's sufficient. If you believe that God heals, that's enough to see the dead raised—as long as you don't submit to all of the negativism, doubt, and unbelief that comes from your senses.

"THIS KIND"

And Jesus said unto them, Because of your unbelief: for verily I say unto you, If ye have faith as a grain of mustard seed, ye shall say unto this mountain, Remove hence to yonder place; and it shall remove; and nothing shall be impossible unto you. [21] Howbeit this kind [of unbelief] goeth not out but by prayer and fasting.

Matthew 17:20-21, brackets mine

Traditionally, people have taught that *"this kind"* refers to a demon that would only go out by prayer and fasting. People will talk about how this is a "strong" demon: "It's a big problem, and we need to fast and pray before we deal with it. We also need to call the prayer chain because just one person isn't going to get this done. We'll need hundreds of people agreeing to be able to see this come out." Some people think that God is limited and that if we ask Him for this, all the lights in heaven are going to dim. Not true!

This scripture is not saying that certain demons are stronger than others. Neither is it saying that certain demons won't respond to Jesus and faith in His name, that you also have to add fasting and prayer to it. That's not what this is talking about!

The subject of the sentence in verse 20 is unbelief. It was their unbelief that was the problem. Therefore, this kind of unbelief only goes out by prayer and fasting (Matt. 17:21). It doesn't take a huge faith—just a simple faith. However, there are some types of unbelief that are hard to deal with; it takes fasting and prayer to get them out.

IGNORANCE, WRONG TEACHING, AND NATURAL

Unbelief can come from ignorance—lack of knowledge. Some people have never heard about miracles. They've never read the Bible. They were brought up in a natural world. They've been taught from the time they were kids that the physical realm is all there is. They've been taught that there isn't a spiritual world or anything beyond the natural realm. That ignorance is unbelief, and it will hinder faith. We could come to that person and tell them about the Word of God, yet there would be a resistance just because they've never heard of or known this before. The antidote to this kind of unbelief is simply to tell them the truth. If they embrace it over a period of time, the truth will set them free.

And ye shall know the truth, and the truth shall make you free.

John 8:32

The second type of unbelief is one that comes through wrong teaching. It's not a lack of knowledge, but wrong knowledge. I was brought up in this. I was taught that miracles passed away with the apostles and that God doesn't do them today. That's the kind of wrong teaching that made me resistant to miracles and believing God for them.

The antidote for this type of unbelief is the same—telling people the truth. Now, ignorance is easier to overcome than wrong teaching; i.e., disbelief. We have to get the wrong teaching out and then start the process of embracing the right teaching. It's more difficult, but it's basically the same process—we tell someone the truth and it will set them free if they believe it.

But the third kind of unbelief—natural unbelief—comes through the five senses. It was this type of natural unbelief that Jesus was talking about in the case of the demonized boy.

> *Then Jesus answered and said, O faithless and perverse generation, how long shall I be with you? how long shall I suffer you? bring him hither to me. [18] And Jesus rebuked the devil; and he departed out of him: and the child was cured from that very hour. [19] Then came the disciples to Jesus apart, and said, Why could not we cast him out? [20] And Jesus said unto them, Because of your unbelief: for verily I say unto you, If ye have faith as a grain of mustard seed, ye shall say unto this mountain, Remove hence to yonder place; and it shall remove; and nothing shall be impossible unto you. [21] Howbeit this kind goeth not out but by prayer and fasting.*
>
> Matthew 17:17-21

When they brought this boy to Jesus, he fell to the ground, wallowed, and foamed at the mouth (Mark 9:20). Apparently the disciples had seen demons cast out before, but they hadn't seen a manifestation quite like this. Their senses—what they saw and heard—began giving them thoughts, feelings, and emotions contrary to what God had promised them.

In essence, the Lord had said, "You can cast out devils. I give you power over all demons."

> *And when he had called unto him his twelve disciples, he gave them power against unclean spirits, to cast them out, and to heal all manner of sickness and all manner of disease.*
>
> Matthew 10:1

> *Then he called his twelve disciples together, and gave them power and authority over all devils, and to cure diseases.*
>
> Luke 9:1

The disciples spoke, but what they saw and heard made it look like this demon wasn't going to respond. So, they had unbelief come through their senses. They had faith, which is why they spoke and were perplexed about not seeing the healing come to pass, but they were still too sensitive to their physical senses.

SIXTH SENSE

Your five senses aren't evil. God gave them to you for good things. You need your five physical senses to function in this world. It's hard to get around if you can't see. If you were to take me somewhere in your car, I'd want you to be able to go by what you see. I wouldn't want you to drive by faith. I'd want you to use your five senses!

However, at times, God will call on all of us to do things that are contrary to our five physical senses. When the Lord calls on us to do something that counters our five senses, how will we respond? The answer to that question depends largely upon our relationship with God. Have we been spending time with Him, specifically in prayer and fasting? We need to spend time receiving from the spirit realm. That way, we will develop our "sixth sense." Then our minds can be trained to respond to faith the same way they respond to our five senses.

TRAIN YOUR MIND

But strong meat belongeth to them...who by reason of use have their senses exercised to discern both good and evil.

Hebrews 5:14

Your five senses can be exercised to discern things beyond just their physical, natural ability. You can get to where you develop this sixth sense of faith. If someone is blind, does that mean that they are just paralyzed and can't move, that they don't do anything because they can't see where they're going? No! They start learning to depend on their other senses more: what they can smell, feel, and hear. They'll use a cane or a guide dog to get around. They'll memorize a route through the house. Their mind will compensate for the lack of sight by depending even more on their other senses.

If you spend time with the Lord in fasting and prayer, you can train your mind to respond to faith. If you spend a lot of time with the Lord, you'll start seeing miracles. You'll see God deliver you in some way or another. You'll start hearing from God and have evidence of the reality of the spiritual world. You'll have physical proof that the Word of God works, and over a period of time, faith will become like a sixth sense to you.

So, even if you can't physically perceive something that is consistent with what you're believing for, your mind can be trained to say, "Well, I can't see, taste, hear, smell, or feel it, but I've spent so much time with the Lord and seen Him come through on so many occasions that I'm aware there is more." That's this sixth sense. You can get to where you rely on faith like a blind person relies on hearing and feeling to still be mobile and get around. You can get to where you aren't limited to your five senses. But it doesn't happen easily.

OUTLINE

I. Miracles don't require huge faith—just a pure and simple faith.

    A. When the disciples asked Jesus to increase their faith, He responded in Luke 17 very much the same as in Mark 11.

    And the apostles said unto the Lord, Increase our faith. [6] And the Lord said, If ye had faith as a grain of mustard seed, ye might say unto this sycamine tree, Be thou plucked up by the root, and be thou planted in the sea; and it should obey you.

                                                              Luke 17:5-6

    B. In other words, Jesus was saying, "Guys, you don't need more faith. Your faith is sufficient."

    C. The problem isn't that you don't have enough faith—it's the fact that you aren't using what you already have (Luke 17:7-8)!

    D. If you could understand this, it would answer some of the questions you've had, questions like, "I know I believed, so why didn't it work?"

    E. It's not because you weren't believing; it's because you were believing and disbelieving at the same time!

    F. If you believe that God heals, that's enough to see the dead raised—as long as you don't submit to all of the negativism, doubt, and unbelief that come from your senses.

II. Traditionally, people have taught that *"this kind"* (Matt. 17:20-21) refers to a demon that would only go out by prayer and fasting:

    And Jesus said unto them, Because of your unbelief: for verily I say unto you, If ye have faith as a grain of mustard seed, ye shall say unto this mountain, Remove hence to yonder place; and it shall remove; and nothing shall be impossible unto you. [21] Howbeit this kind [of unbelief] goeth not out but by prayer and fasting.

                                                             Brackets mine

    A. This scripture is not saying that certain demons are stronger than others.

    B. Neither is it saying that certain demons won't respond to Jesus and faith in His name.

C. The subject of the sentence in verse 20 is unbelief; it was their unbelief that was the problem.

D. There are some types of unbelief that are hard to deal with; it takes fasting and prayer to get them out (Matt. 17:21).

III. Unbelief can come from ignorance—lack of knowledge.

A. Some people have been taught that there isn't a spiritual world or anything beyond the natural realm.

B. That ignorance is unbelief, and it will hinder faith.

C. The antidote to this kind of unbelief is simply to tell them the truth.

D. If they embrace it over a period of time, the truth will set them free:

And ye shall know the truth, and the truth shall make you free.
                                                                    John 8:32

IV. The second type of unbelief is one that comes through wrong teaching.

A. It's not a lack of knowledge, but wrong knowledge.

B. The antidote for this type of unbelief is the same—telling people the truth.

C. We have to get the wrong teaching out and then start the process of embracing the right teaching.

D. We tell someone the truth, and it will set them free if they believe it.

V. The third kind of unbelief—natural unbelief—comes through the five senses.

A. It was this type of natural unbelief that Jesus was talking about in the case of the demonized boy (Matt. 17:17-21).

B. Apparently the disciples had seen demons cast out before, but they hadn't seen a manifestation quite like that (Mark 9:20).

C. Their senses—what they saw and heard—began giving them thoughts, feelings, and emotions contrary to what God had promised them (Matt. 10:1 and Luke 9:1).

D. They had faith, which is why they spoke and were perplexed about not seeing the healing come to pass, but they were still too sensitive to their physical senses.

VI. Your five senses aren't evil—God gave them to you for good things.

   A. You need your five physical senses to function in this world.

   B. However, at times, God will call on you to do things that are contrary to your five physical senses.

   C. You need to spend time receiving from the spirit realm; that way, you will develop your "sixth sense."

   D. Then your mind can be trained to respond to faith the same way it responds to your five senses.

VII. Your five senses can be exercised to discern things beyond just their physical, natural ability to where you develop this sixth sense of faith.

   But strong meat belongeth to them...who by reason of use have their senses exercised to discern both good and evil.

   Hebrews 5:14

   A. If you spend time with the Lord in fasting and prayer, you can train your mind to respond to faith.

   B. You'll have physical proof that the Word of God works, and over a period of time, faith will become like a sixth sense to you.

   C. You can get to where you rely on faith like a blind person relies on hearing and feeling to still be mobile and get around.

   D. You can get to where you aren't limited to your five senses—but it doesn't happen easily.

TEACHER'S GUIDE

1. Miracles don't require huge faith—just a pure and simple faith. When the disciples asked Jesus to increase their faith, He responded in Luke 17 very much the same as in Mark 11.

> *And the apostles said unto the Lord, Increase our faith. [6] And the Lord said, If ye had faith as a grain of mustard seed, ye might say unto this sycamine tree, Be thou plucked up by the root, and be thou planted in the sea; and it should obey you.*
>
> Luke 17:5-6

In other words, Jesus was saying, "Guys, you don't need more faith. Your faith is sufficient." The problem isn't that we don't have enough faith—it's the fact that we aren't using what we already have (Luke 17:7-8)! If we could understand this, it would answer some of the questions we've had, questions like, "I know I believed, so why didn't it work?" It's not because we weren't believing; it's because we were believing and disbelieving at the same time! If we believe that God heals, that's enough to see the dead raised—as long as we don't submit to all of the negativism, doubt, and unbelief that come from our senses.

1a. What kind of faith do miracles require?

A pure and simple faith

1b. When the apostles asked Jesus to increase their faith, He basically said that _____.
   A. Their faith was already sufficient
   B. He was angry
   C. He had been waiting for them to ask
   D. All of the above
   E. None of the above

A. Their faith was already sufficient

1c. Faith doesn't work when you are _____ and _____ at the same time.

Believing / disbelieving

2. Traditionally, people have taught that *"this kind"* (Matt. 17:20-21) refers to a demon that would only go out by prayer and fasting:

> *And Jesus said unto them, Because of your unbelief: for verily I say unto you, If ye have faith as a grain of mustard seed, ye shall say unto this mountain, Remove hence to yonder place; and it shall remove;*

and nothing shall be impossible unto you. [21] *Howbeit this kind* [of unbelief] *goeth not out but by prayer and fasting.*

Brackets mine

This scripture is not saying that certain demons are stronger than others. Neither is it saying that certain demons won't respond to Jesus and faith in His name. The subject of the sentence in verse 20 is unbelief; it was their unbelief that was the problem. There are some types of unbelief that are hard to deal with; it takes fasting and prayer to get them out (Matt. 17:21).

2a. True or false: The *"this kind"* described in Matthew 17:21 refers to an especially difficult demon.
   False

2b. There are some types of _____ that only go out by prayer and fasting.
   Unbelief

2c. *Discussion question:* Why do you think Jesus said prayer and fasting instead of some other solution?
   Discussion question

3. Unbelief can come from ignorance—lack of knowledge. Some people have been taught that there isn't a spiritual world or anything beyond the natural realm. That ignorance is unbelief, and it will hinder faith. The antidote to this kind of unbelief is simply to tell them the truth. If they embrace it over a period of time, the truth will set them free:

   And ye shall know the truth, and the truth shall make you free.

   John 8:32

3a. True or false: Some people lack the knowledge that a spiritual world exists.
   True

3b. *Discussion question:* In what areas of your life have you experienced unbelief due to ignorance, or lack of knowledge?
   Discussion question

4. The second type of unbelief is one that comes through wrong teaching. It's not a lack of knowledge, but wrong knowledge. The antidote for this type of unbelief is the same—telling people the truth. We have to get the wrong teaching out and then start the process of embracing the right teaching. We tell someone the truth, and it will set them free if they believe it.

4a. True or false: Another type of unbelief is a result of wrong teaching.
    True
4b. *Discussion question:* In what areas of your life have you had to overcome unbelief due to wrong teaching?
    Discussion question

5. The third kind of unbelief—natural unbelief—comes through the five senses. It was this type of natural unbelief that Jesus was talking about in the case of the demonized boy (Matt. 17:17-21). Apparently the disciples had seen demons cast out before, but they hadn't seen a manifestation quite like that (Mark 9:20). Their senses—what they saw and heard—began giving them thoughts, feelings, and emotions contrary to what God had promised them (Matt. 10:1 and Luke 9:1). They had faith, which is why they spoke and were perplexed about not seeing the healing come to pass, but they were still too sensitive to their physical senses.

5a. A third kind of unbelief comes through your senses and is called

    _____ _____.

    Natural unbelief
5b. What can natural unbelief cause that makes it harder to believe?
    A. Thoughts and feelings
    B. Emotions contrary to the promises of God
    C. Faith
    D. A and B
    E. B and C
    D. A and B
5c. *Discussion question:* How have your physical senses come against your faith?
    Discussion question

6. Our five senses aren't evil—God gave them to us for good things. We need our five physical senses to function in this world. However, at times, God will call on us to do things that are contrary to our five physical senses. We need to spend time receiving from the spirit realm; that way, we will develop our "sixth sense." Then our minds can be trained to respond to faith the same way they respond to our five senses.

6a. True or false: Your five senses are evil.
    False
6b. *Discussion question:* In what ways can you spend time receiving from the spiritual realm and develop your "sixth sense"?
    Discussion question

7. Our five senses can be exercised to discern things beyond just their physical, natural ability to where we develop this sixth sense of faith.

> *But strong meat belongeth to them...who by reason of use have their senses exercised to discern both good and evil.*
>
> Hebrews 5:14

If we spend time with the Lord in fasting and prayer, we can train our minds to respond to faith. We'll have physical proof that the Word of God works, and over a period of time, faith will become like a sixth sense to us. We can get to where we rely on faith like a blind person relies on hearing and feeling to still be mobile and get around. We can get to where we aren't limited to our five senses—but it doesn't happen easily.

7a. *Discussion question:* How is faith like a "sixth sense"?
     Discussion question

7b. *Discussion question:* Why is it not easy to get to where you aren't limited to your five senses?
     Discussion question

DISCIPLESHIP QUESTIONS

1. What kind of faith do miracles require?

    _____

    _____

    _____

2. When the apostles asked Jesus to increase their faith, He basically said that _____.
    A. Their faith was already sufficient
    B. He was angry
    C. He had been waiting for them to ask
    D. All of the above
    E. None of the above

3. Faith doesn't work when you are _____ and _____ at the same time.

4. True or false: The "this kind" described in Matthew 17:21 refers to an especially difficult demon.

5. There are some types of _____ that only go out by prayer and fasting.

6. *Discussion question:* Why do you think Jesus said prayer and fasting instead of some other solution?

    _____

    _____

    _____

7. True or false: Some people lack the knowledge that a spiritual world exists.

8. *Discussion question:* In what areas of your life have you experienced unbelief due to ignorance, or lack of knowledge?

    _____

    _____

    _____

9. True or false: Another type of unbelief is a result of wrong teaching.

10. *Discussion question:* In what areas of your life have you had to overcome unbelief due to wrong teaching?

    _____

    _____

    _____

11. A third kind of unbelief comes through your senses and is called
    _____ _____.

12. What can natural unbelief cause that makes it harder to believe?
    A.   Thoughts and feelings
    B.   Emotions contrary to the promises of God
    C.   Faith
    D.   A and B
    E.   B and C

13. *Discussion question:* How have your physical senses come against your faith?

    _____

    _____

    _____

14. True or false: Your five senses are evil.

15. *Discussion question:* In what ways can you spend time receiving from the spiritual realm and develop your "sixth sense"?

_____

_____

_____

16. *Discussion question:* How is faith like a "sixth sense"?

_____

_____

_____

17. *Discussion question:* Why is it not easy to get to where you aren't limited to your five senses?

_____

_____

_____

ANSWER KEY

1. A pure and simple faith

2. A. Their faith was already sufficient

3. Believing / disbelieving

4. False

5. Unbelief

6. *Discussion question*

7. True

8. *Discussion question*

9. True

10. *Discussion question*

11. Natural unbelief

12. D. A and B

13. *Discussion question*

14. False

15. *Discussion question*

16. *Discussion question*

17. *Discussion question*

SCRIPTURES

LUKE 17:5-8

And the apostles said unto the Lord, Increase our faith. [6] And the Lord said, If ye had faith as a grain of mustard seed, ye might say unto this sycamine tree, Be thou plucked up by the root, and be thou planted in the sea; and it should obey you. [7] But which of you, having a servant plowing or feeding cattle, will say unto him by and by, when he is come from the field, Go and sit down to meat? [8] And will not rather say unto him, Make ready wherewith I may sup, and gird thyself, and serve me, till I have eaten and drunken; and afterward thou shalt eat and drink?

MATTHEW 17:17-21

Then Jesus answered and said, O faithless and perverse generation, how long shall I be with you? how long shall I suffer you? bring him hither to me. [18] And Jesus rebuked the devil; and he departed out of him: and the child was cured from that very hour. [19] Then came the disciples to Jesus apart, and said, Why could not we cast him out? [20] And Jesus said unto them, Because of your unbelief: for verily I say unto you, If ye have faith as a grain of mustard seed, ye shall say unto this mountain, Remove hence to yonder place; and it shall remove; and nothing shall be impossible unto you. [21] Howbeit this kind goeth not out but by prayer and fasting.

JOHN 8:32

And ye shall know the truth, and the truth shall make you free.

MARK 9:20

And they brought him unto him: and when he saw him, straightway the spirit tare him; and he fell on the ground, and wallowed foaming.

MATTHEW 10:1

And when he had called unto him his twelve disciples, he gave them power against unclean spirits, to cast them out, and to heal all manner of sickness and all manner of disease.

LUKE 9:1

Then he called his twelve disciples together, and gave them power and authority over all devils, and to cure diseases.

HEBREWS 5:14

But strong meat belongeth to them that are of full age, even those who by reason of use have their senses exercised to discern both good and evil.

EXERCISE YOURSELF

LESSON 15

But strong meat belongeth to them that are of full age, even those who by reason of use have their senses exercised to discern both good and evil.

Hebrews 5:14

Notice that Hebrews 5:14 says that their senses were exercised *"by reason of use."* In other words, you have to exercise. This word *"exercised"* is very important. You don't just get up and start preparing for a marathon the morning of the race. I actually trained for a marathon once, and I didn't even make it. I ran half a marathon—13.1 miles—and it took me nearly a year to prepare to do that! People who prepare for, run in, and win marathons train for multiple years to get there. You can't start training the morning of the race. You have to exercise yourself!

Many Christians don't really spend much time with God. They live in the physical realm, working a job and watching television. They do everything in the natural realm, spending virtually no time praying and fellowshipping with God or fasting and denying their senses. Then they get into some crisis situation and give it all they have. They're 100 percent sincere and genuinely dedicated, but it's too little, too late. They haven't exercised themselves. Some people even die, not because they were believing wrong, but because their senses had too much control over them.

This is why fasting works. Fasting is simply a denying of the five senses. Our taste, or appetite, is one of the strongest senses we have. People have actually murdered over food. I remember reading a story once about a group of people who were on their way west to California in the 1800s and ran into a blizzard. The children ate their mothers. They found them cannibalizing their own kin because of the desire for food. It's a strong, strong desire, and it doesn't take very long before it manifests. If we're just dominated and controlled by our five senses, if they are more real to us than what God says, and if that sixth sense of faith isn't the strongest, most dominant sense we have, fasting is how we can change that.

WHO'S CONTROLLING WHOM?

Within just a few hours of when you start fasting, your appetite will begin complaining and trying to regain control. It will try to dominate and force you to eat. If you stick with it and say "Nope, I'm going to believe God. Man does not live by bread alone, but by every word that proceeds from the mouth of God" (Matt. 4:4) and if that's your attitude and you persist, your body will rebel. It will try to control you.

If you just continue saying "Well then, I'm going to fast all day," your appetite will respond "All day? I'll be dead by evening!"

If you answer "All right, we'll go two days," your body will reply "No, I'll never last two days!"

"All right, three days!"

Pretty soon, your appetite will learn that it's going to survive, so it will have to submit. When you fast over a prolonged period of time, after about two or three days of denying your appetite, you actually reach a place where you aren't hungry anymore. It doesn't bother you. You can get to a place where you aren't missing it anymore, because your appetite is under control.

Then if sickness attacks your body, you can say, "I'm healed in the name of Jesus." If your body doesn't instantaneously manifest that healing and you're still in pain, you can tell your body, "I'm not going by what I feel." If you've been fasting and praying—denying yourself and spending time in the presence of God—you've trained yourself to say, "What I believe is just as real as what I see, taste, hear, smell, and feel." Your body will respond to that. You'll be able to go on, stay the course, and stand until you see the manifestation of your healing.

But if you haven't been spending time in the spiritual realm, if you've just been totally occupied and dominated by the physical realm, and you say "Body, you're healed. I don't care what you feel. By the stripes of Jesus I was healed," your senses will answer with "Who are you to tell me anything? I tell you when to eat, what to eat, and how much to eat." Since you haven't exercised your senses, they'll control you, instead of you controlling them.

SENSITIZED TO GOD

You can't avoid the natural type of unbelief that comes from what you see, taste, hear, smell, and feel. That's not an ignorance problem. It's not a renewing-your-mind problem. It's just that you are spending more time in the physical world than you are in the spiritual world. You have to reverse that. You must get to where you are focused on the Lord and His Word.

When Peter was focused on Jesus, he didn't have any problems, because he wasn't considering anything contrary to faith. But when he took his attention off of Jesus, he began to sink. Peter had already covered most of the distance. Jesus didn't have to run to him and grab him. The Lord just reached out and took hold of him. Peter was close enough to almost touch Jesus. Once he felt like he'd nearly made it, he relaxed. He took his attention off the Lord and began to look at the wind and the waves. When he did that, he started sinking.

> *But when he saw the wind boisterous, he was afraid; and beginning to sink, he cried, saying, Lord, save me. [31] And immediately Jesus stretched forth his hand, and caught him, and said unto him, O thou of little faith, wherefore didst thou doubt?*
>
> Matthew 14:30-31

You can't afford to take your eyes off Jesus! Spend time in the Word and prayer, denying your five senses and fellowshipping with God. When you pray, your five senses are going to ask, "Who are you talking to? I can't see anybody. I can't hear anyone. I don't feel anybody here." But if you persist in prayer and relationship with God, you'll begin to experience miracles. There will be tangible proof that God is there and that He's talking to you. After a while, your senses will say "Oh, there's another sense that I wasn't aware of. Whatever faith says is true," and you'll get to where your senses will bow and yield to faith. When you spend time in the presence of the Lord, your heart becomes sensitive to Him. It's just that simple!

Peter was able to walk on the water because he got out of the boat. He started walking to Jesus. As long as he kept his eyes on the Lord, he was fine. But once he took his eyes off Jesus, unbelief came. Peter still had faith, but unbelief started coming by his considering natural things.

All of us have natural things that are going to tell us that the Word of God doesn't work. If you can't see, taste, hear, smell, or feel it, your senses will try to convince you that it doesn't exist. You are going to have to train and exercise yourself to know there's more to it than that. There is no way to do this except through spending quantity time in the presence of God through fasting and prayer.

GO ALL THE WAY!

> *Howbeit this kind* [of unbelief] *goeth not out but by prayer and fasting.*
> Matthew 17:21, brackets mine

Prayer and fasting is the only way to deal with natural unbelief. You can get rid of the other two types of unbelief—ignorance and disbelief—just by hearing the truth and believing it. But the only way you can overcome your five senses and the unbelief they feed you is through fasting and prayer, spending time in God's presence. Be more at home in the spiritual world than you are in the physical. Get to where you believe that the spiritual world exists more than you believe what you can see, taste, hear, smell, and feel. You can exercise yourself to that point, but it's going to take some time and effort. You can't wait until the morning of your trial to overcome this kind of unbelief. You just need to get focused on God and not look to the right or the left.

We let so much occupy us—television, radio, books, magazines—all kinds of things. In their place, they're okay. But when you are walking on water, you need to keep your eyes on Jesus. When you're out there believing God for a miracle, you can't afford to look to the right or the left. You have to keep your eyes straight before you, not turned to either side. If you do that, not only can you be a water walker, but you can also walk all the way to the other shore. You don't have to stop or fall. You can continue all the way to your God-ordained destination!

Your faith is sufficient. God gave you enough faith. It's not that you have less than what you need. Actually, you have more than what you need—more unbelief! Once you close the door on that unbelief, you will walk on water!

OUTLINE

I. Notice that Hebrews 5:14 says that their senses were exercised *"by reason of use"*:

> *But strong meat belongeth to them that are of full age, even those who*
> *by reason of use have their senses exercised to discern both good*
> *and evil.*
>
> Hebrews 5:14

A. In other words, you have to exercise.

B. You don't just get up and start preparing for a marathon the morning of the race.

C. Many Christians do everything in the natural realm, spending virtually no time praying and fellowshipping with God or fasting and denying their senses—then they get into some crisis situation and give it all they have.

D. They're 100 percent sincere and genuinely dedicated, but it's too little, too late.

E. Some people even die, not because they were believing wrong, but because their senses had too much control over them.

II. Fasting is simply a denying of the five senses.

A. If you're controlled by your five senses and that sixth sense of faith isn't the most dominant sense you have, fasting is how you can change that.

B. When you start fasting, your appetite will begin complaining and trying to regain control; but if you persist, your appetite will learn to submit.

C. Then if sickness attacks your body, you've trained yourself to say, "What I believe is just as real as what I see, taste, hear, smell, and feel."

D. You'll be able to stand until you see the manifestation of your healing.

E. But if you haven't been spending time in the spiritual realm, if you've just been totally occupied and dominated by the physical realm, your senses will control you, instead of you controlling them.

III. You must get to where you are focused on the Lord and His Word.

    A. When Peter was focused on Jesus, he didn't have any problems, because he wasn't considering anything contrary to faith; but once he felt like he'd nearly made it, he took his attention off of the Lord and started sinking (Matt. 14:30-31).

    B. You can't afford to take your eyes off Jesus!

    C. Spend time in the Word and prayer, denying your five senses and fellowshipping with God.

    D. There will be tangible proof that God is there and that He's talking to you.

    E. When you spend time in the presence of the Lord, your heart becomes sensitive to Him.

IV. Prayer and fasting is the only way to deal with natural unbelief:

Howbeit this kind [of unbelief] *goeth not out but by prayer and fasting.*
Matthew 17:21, brackets mine

    A. You can get rid of the other two types of unbelief—ignorance and disbelief—just by hearing the truth and believing it.

    B. But the only way you can overcome your five senses and the unbelief they feed you is through fasting and prayer, spending time in God's presence.

    C. You can't wait until the morning of your trial to overcome this kind of unbelief.

    D. When you're believing God for a miracle and keep your eyes straight before you, not only can you be a water walker, but you can also walk all the way to the other shore!

TEACHER'S GUIDE

1. We need to notice that Hebrews 5:14 says that their senses were exercised *"by reason of use"*:

> *But strong meat belongeth to them that are of full age, even those who by reason of use have their senses exercised to discern both good and evil.*
>
> Hebrews 5:14

In other words, we have to exercise. We don't just get up and start preparing for a marathon the morning of the race. Many Christians do everything in the natural realm, spending virtually no time praying and fellowshipping with God or fasting and denying their senses—then they get into some crisis situation and give it all they have. They're 100 percent sincere and genuinely dedicated, but it's too little, too late. Some people even die, not because they were believing wrong, but because their senses had too much control over them.

1a. True or false: Hebrews 5:14 says that their senses were exercised by grace alone.
    False
1b. Some people die because of what?
    Because their senses had too much control over them
1c. *Discussion question:* Besides fasting, what are some ways you can exercise your senses?
    Discussion question

2. Fasting is simply a denying of the five senses. If we're controlled by our five senses and that sixth sense of faith isn't the most dominant sense we have, fasting is how we can change that. When we start fasting, our appetite will begin complaining and trying to regain control; but if we persist, our appetite will learn to submit. Then if sickness attacks our bodies, we've trained ourselves to say, "What I believe is just as real as what I see, taste, hear, smell, and feel." We'll be able to stand until we see the manifestation of our healing. But if we haven't been spending time in the spiritual realm, if we've just been totally occupied and dominated by the physical realm, our senses will control us, instead of us controlling them.

2a. If you persist in fasting, your appetite will learn to _____.
    A. Dominate your senses
    B. Submit
    C. Manipulate you
    D. All of the above
    E. None of the above
    B. Submit

2b. Fasting trains you to say what?

"What I believe is just as real as what I see, taste, hear, smell, and feel"

2c. *Discussion question:* What other battles besides sickness do you think fasting prepares you for?

Discussion question

3. We must get to where we are focused on the Lord and His Word. When Peter was focused on Jesus, he didn't have any problems, because he wasn't considering anything contrary to faith; but once he felt like he'd nearly made it, he took his attention off of the Lord and started sinking (Matt. 14:30-31). We can't afford to take our eyes off Jesus! We need to spend time in the Word and prayer, denying our five senses and fellowshipping with God. There will be tangible proof that God is there and that He's talking to us. When we spend time in the presence of the Lord, our hearts become sensitive to Him.

3a. True or false: You must get to where you are focused on your circumstances.

False

3b. Why is that when Peter was focused on Jesus, he didn't have any problems?

He wasn't considering anything contrary to faith

3c. What happens when you spend time in the presence of the Lord?

Your heart becomes sensitive to Him

3d. *Discussion question:* What are some ways you can focus on the Lord and His Word?

Discussion question

4. Prayer and fasting is the only way to deal with natural unbelief:

> *Howbeit this kind* [of unbelief] *goeth not out but by prayer and fasting.*
> Matthew 17:21, brackets mine

We can get rid of the other two types of unbelief—ignorance and disbelief—just by hearing the truth and believing it. But the only way we can overcome our five senses and the unbelief they feed us is through fasting and prayer, spending time in God's presence. We can't wait until the morning of our trials to overcome this kind of unbelief. When we're believing God for miracles and keep our eyes straight before us, not only can we be water walkers, but we can also walk all the way to the other shore!

4a. You _____ wait until the morning of your _____ to overcome this kind of _____.

Can't / trial / unbelief

4b. *Discussion question:* What would it look like for you to walk all the way to the other shore?

Discussion question

DISCIPLESHIP QUESTIONS

1.   True or false: Hebrews 5:14 says that their senses were exercised by grace alone.

2.   Some people die because of what?

_____

_____

_____

3.   *Discussion question:* Besides fasting, what are some ways you can exercise your senses?

_____

_____

_____

4.   If you persist in fasting, your appetite will learn to _____.
     A.   Dominate your senses
     B.   Submit
     C.   Manipulate you
     D.   All of the above
     E.   None of the above

5.   Fasting trains you to say what?

_____

_____

_____

6.   *Discussion question:* What other battles besides sickness do you think fasting prepares you for?

_____

_____

_____

7. True or false: You must get to where you are focused on your circumstances.

8. Why is that when Peter was focused on Jesus, he didn't have any problems?

    _____

    _____

    _____

9. What happens when you spend time in the presence of the Lord?

    _____

    _____

    _____

10. *Discussion question:* What are some ways you can focus on the Lord and His Word?

    _____

    _____

    _____

11. You _____ wait until the morning of your _____ to overcome this kind of _____.

12. *Discussion question:* What would it look like for you to walk all the way to the other shore?

    _____

    _____

    _____

ANSWER KEY

1. False

2. Because their senses had too much control over them

3. *Discussion question*

4. B. Submit

5. "What I believe is just as real as what I see, taste, hear, smell, and feel"

6. *Discussion question*

7. False

8. He wasn't considering anything contrary to faith

9. Your heart becomes sensitive to Him

10. *Discussion question*

11. Can't / trial / unbelief

12. *Discussion question*

SCRIPTURES

HEBREWS 5:14

But strong meat belongeth to them that are of full age, even those who by reason of use have their senses exercised to discern both good and evil.

MATTHEW 4:4

But he answered and said, It is written, Man shall not live by bread alone, but by every word that proceedeth out of the mouth of God.

MATTHEW 14:30-31

But when he saw the wind boisterous, he was afraid; and beginning to sink, he cried, saying, Lord, save me. [31] And immediately Jesus stretched forth his hand, and caught him, and said unto him, O thou of little faith, wherefore didst thou doubt?

MATTHEW 17:21

Howbeit this kind goeth not out but by prayer and fasting.

Receive Jesus as Your Savior

Choosing to receive Jesus Christ as your Lord and Savior is the most important decision you'll ever make!

God's Word promises, *"That if thou shalt confess with thy mouth the Lord Jesus, and shalt believe in thine heart that God hath raised him from the dead, thou shalt be saved. [10] For with the heart man believeth unto righteousness; and with the mouth confession is made unto salvation"* (Rom. 10:9-10). *"For whosoever shall call upon the name of the Lord shall be saved"* (Rom. 10:13).

By His grace, God has already done everything to provide salvation. Your part is simply to believe and receive.

Pray out loud, "Jesus, I confess that You are my Lord and Savior. I believe in my heart that God raised You from the dead. By faith in Your Word, I receive salvation now. Thank You for saving me!"

The very moment you commit your life to Jesus Christ, the truth of His Word instantly comes to pass in your spirit. Now that you're born again, there's a brand-new you!

Please contact me and let me know that you've prayed to receive Jesus as your Savior or to be filled with the Holy Spirit. I would like to rejoice with you and help you understand more fully what has taken place in your life. I'll send you a free gift that will help you understand and grow in your new relationship with the Lord. *Welcome to your new life!*

RECEIVE THE HOLY SPIRIT

As His child, your loving heavenly Father wants to give you the supernatural power you need to live this new life.

"For every one that asketh receiveth; and he that seeketh findeth; and to him that knocketh it shall be opened.... [13] How much more shall your heavenly Father give the Holy Spirit to them that ask him?" (Luke 11:10 and 13b).

All you have to do is ask, believe, and receive!

Pray, "Father, I recognize my need for Your power to live this new life. Please fill me with Your Holy Spirit. By faith, I receive it right now! Thank You for baptizing me. Holy Spirit, You are welcome in my life!"

Congratulations—now you're filled with God's supernatural power!

Some syllables from a language you don't recognize will rise up from your heart to your mouth (1 Cor. 14:14). As you speak them out loud by faith, you're releasing God's power from within and building yourself up in your spirit (1 Cor. 14:4). You can do this whenever and wherever you like.

It doesn't really matter whether you felt anything or not when you prayed to receive the Lord and His Spirit. If you believed in your heart that you received, then God's Word promises that you did. *"Therefore I say unto you, What things soever ye desire, when ye pray, believe that ye receive them, and ye shall have them"* (Mark 11:24). God always honors His Word—believe it!

Please contact me and let me know that you've prayed to receive Jesus as your Savior or to be filled with the Holy Spirit. I would like to rejoice with you and help you understand more fully what has taken place in your life. I'll send you a free gift that will help you understand and grow in your new relationship with the Lord. Welcome to your new life!

ABOUT THE AUTHOR

For more than four-and-a-half decades, Andrew has taught God's Word with clarity and simplicity, emphasizing the unconditional love and grace of God. His vision is to spread the Gospel as far and deep as possible through his daily *Gospel Truth* television and radio programs, broadcast nationally and internationally to over half the world's population.

Andrew has an extensive library of teaching materials in print, audio, and video—most of which can be downloaded for free from his website: **www.awmi .net**. To date, Andrew Wommack Ministries has distributed millions of free teaching materials worldwide.

Andrew founded Charis Bible College in 1994 and has established more than forty Charis locations in major American cities and around the world. Over 6,000 students attend classes in person, by correspondence, or online—and that number continues to grow. Graduates are impacting millions of people with whom Andrew may never come in contact. As world changers, these men and women are influencing others for the Gospel and bringing glory to God.

ANDREW'S TEACHING RECOMMENDATIONS IN THIS STUDY GUIDE

LESSON 2

"The Sovereignty of God"

One of the most contested doctrinal beliefs between believers is the sovereignty of God. And unfortunately, an inaccurate view of this causes dysfunction in the Christian life. Listen as Andrew uses the Word of God to eliminate the confusion.

Single CD
Item Code: L03-C

"God's Not Guilty"

Many Christians blame God for any and all problems. Are they at least partly right? Andrew settles the issue with this teaching.

Single CD
Item Code: L04-C

Spiritual Authority

Spiritual authority is an indispensable ingredient in God's recipe for victory. If you don't understand your authority, you will always be waiting on the Lord to do something He told you to do.

CD series
Item Code: 1017-C

LESSON 4

God Wants You Well

In this teaching, Andrew shares the truth of what God's unconditional love and grace have already provided. Healing is a big part of that provision. He answers many common questions, including those about Paul's thorn in the flesh, the sovereignty of God, and more.

CD series	DVD series	Paperback	Study Guide
Item Code: 1036-C	Item Code: 1036-D	Item Code: 330	Item Code: 430